MORE INSTANT PAINTING

MORE

INSTANT PAINTING

A guide for the absolute beginner
The only book with color formulas
in exact amounts

by
Nancy Circelli Kominsky

THE BOBBS-MERRILL COMPANY, INC.
Indianapolis / New York

Acknowledgments

My thanks to all of my friends for their patience and for keeping my nose to the grindstone; to my talented daughter-in-law, Barbara, for the clever cartoons.
I owe special thanks to Joseph De Cosmo, my assistant at our Sunday Painters of Rome Studio, who devised and executed the four large completed drawings. I am grateful for his excellent and pertinent advice in editing the material in the book, and for " minding the store " while I wrote this deathless prose.

N.C.K.

The Bobbs-Merrill Company, Inc.
Publishers　·　Indianapolis　·　New York

First printing

To all my students

CONTENTS

FOREWORD

If you have always wanted to paint but don't know where to start, or you have been painting awhile but hanging your paintings in a closet, then this is the book for you.

More Instant Painting *is similar to* Instant Painting, *written for the absolute beginner, but naturally the projects in* More Instant Painting *are a little more advanced (don't panic, please keep reading). This book also uses the same simplified stroke-by-stroke methodical approach to painting that guarantees those longed-for instant results.*

It is very likely that in sheer desperation you've bought one "How To" painting book after another or have been changing classes and teachers in the hope that one would point your nose in the right direction. You have discovered there is nothing more frustrating and discouraging than to attend painting classes with the current "non-teaching" teachers, particularly if you're an absolute beginner and don't even know where to start. One teacher had the class painting circles until "something happened." (I understand they are still painting great *circles). And another simply sat, drank coffee and smoked all during class. His method of instruction consisted solely of these words — "Do whatever you'd like to do." After three hysterical hours and the canvas a messy glob, you know what you'd like to do...only it's not dignified!*

Then too, there are always those who are convinced that the ability to paint is something you are born with like blue eyes or red hair. They harbor the wild or romantic notion that one, in a frenzy of inspiration, rushes to the canvas (obviously a little elf has prepared the palette, canvas, etc., etc.) and feverishly executes a masterpiece. Naturally one never *paints unless one is in the mood.* Forget it! It just isn't so!

With discipline and a few simple rules, painting is an art that can be achieved much in the same way one learns to play a musical instrument, sew, drive, golf or what have you. (This creates anguished screams of "prostituting" art in the art world.) I have received hundreds of enthusiastic letters from all over the country and abroad from happy novices who have enjoyed tremendous success with Instant Painting.

These beginning painters have proved beyond a doubt that: (A) everyone without exception has innate creative ability and therefore can learn to paint, and, (B) by following the simplified instructions for drawing and color formulas, this method is instantly productive...and eliminates confusion and despair.

In 1962 "The Sunday Painters Art Studio" was launched in Burbank, California, when a friend talked me into teaching oil painting to women who were bored with household and club routine and who were dropouts from bridge and golf. (As one who trumps her partner's ace and shoots ninety in golf all in one hole, *it figures...no one* will *play with you.) I was skeptical at first, but an artist's income is spasmodic at best, and although I'm not the "bread and cheese in the attic" type of starving artist, a two-bath duplex dosen't change the situation. As a matter of fact, a great many well-known painters spend some of their time teaching. It's not always true that those* who can't...teach!

So when I decided to teach I realized that for all practical purposes the students I would attract would not be interested in career painting and didn't have the time or patience to go the whole bit. I thought back to my own art training and what I didn't like or find practical while learning. First: a lack of basic elementary rules for beginning painters. Therefore, I decided my approach had to be: this is what you do *and* this is how you do it! *Secondly: an overemphasis on drawing. Too much stress on drawing results in a tight, dull, muddy painting because one ends up trying to color a drawing. If you have a* good *drawing and* poor *color you do* not *have a painting, but a poor drawing with good color can be a good painting. For in painting* color *is more important.*

However, color can be the most frustrating problem for the beginning painter. (Nothing is scarier than seeing a palette full of squeezed-out paint if you don't know how to start.) Therefore, Instant Painting *and* More Instant Painting *are the* only books *with specific color formulas, or directions for mixing the* light, medium *and* dark *tones of each of the colors that are used in most painting. In addition, there are formulas for sky, earth, water, rocks, etc., and four background color combinations. A new color chart of Pastel Tints has been added in* More Instant Painting, *with formulas for exact mixing. Most important, these* four *separate color charts (78 different tones) are* interchangeable *and can also be used for* any painting, *not just for the exercises in the books.*

More Instant Painting *has several other innovations which you will find tremendously helpful, plus four new and exciting lessons.*

1. *The palette is shown in full color to help you see the correct tonal value of aqua, mixed green and purple: the three colors that have to be mixed in preparing the palette.*

2. *A new color chart of six pastel tints. Unlike the other color charts, it has an additional tonal value of "Extra-Light" for each tint. (Great for florals, especially.)*

3. *A completely detailed drawing for each painting project in the book, sectioned off with grid lines to help you place the subject correctly on your canvas. (Important with these more advanced projects.)*

4. *Four carefully chosen painting projects as follows:*
   A. Floral — *using all tones of the new pastel tints color chart (it won't be easy but you'll love it).*
   B. Lobster and Wine — *study of glass, porcelain, etc. (It would be nice to use a fresh lobster — I've eaten many a "still life" — but if not, you can probably manage a bottle of wine, and a little sip now and then will give you a more "relaxed" painting.)*
   C. Scottish Seacoast — *landscape introducing simple perspective...a stone house. (This is a painting you will love but I suggest you save some of the wine, especially when painting that storm-tossed sky.)*
   D. Italian Flower Vendor — *introducing simple figures (are they ever?) and*

buildings. (At this point you are entertaining the thought of leaving out the figures. Don't! *You* can *paint them! And what is an Italian street scene* without *Italians?)*

Now relax, start painting and enjoy yourself. But remember, all will not always be sweetness and light. There will be moments when you will feel like chucking the whole thing! Moments when you will be exposed to the "expert" opinions of assorted friends and relatives (suddenly everyone's an art critic). A well-meaning friend purred to one of my students upon viewing her finished *masterpiece: " My dear, it looks like something lovely you are going to finish sometime." But worst of all will be yourself. There will be moments when you will* lack confidence, feel confused *and* be impatient. *If you paint twenty or thirty years, and become another* Van Gogh *or* Matisse, *you will still* lack confidence, feel confused *and* be impatient!*
This is the makeup of the creative personality, and this kind of friction is the honing process for the growth of the creative process. Naturally, this book makes no pretenses about turning out instant masterpieces, *but because this system of painting is* instantly productive *it will not only give you a much needed outlet for your innate creative ability, it will also increase your awareness of your environment and give you much enjoyment.*

Since " The Sunday Painters Art Studio" was launched in Burbank in 1962, it has continued to enjoy the same success the last five years in Rome with international students from dozens of embassies and private companies. This unique system of painting has been introduced through television and lectures both here and abroad, and at present there are projected plans for translation of the books into foreign languages and a possible television teaching series.

" Instant Painting" has truly become international!

MATERIALS
NO SUBSTITUTIONS

1. PAINTS (Grumbacher's Pretested Colors, or other available colors)
    Note: Buy large tubes.

Zinc yellow (lemon yellow)	Yellow ochre
Cadmium orange	Cadmium vermilion
Cadmium yellow medium	Burnt sienna
*Alizarin crimson	Naples yellow
Ultramarine blue	Burnt umber
Thalo green	Zinc white

*Rose madder lake can be substituted for alizarin crimson. Purple, mixed green, and aqua are not purchased, but mixed according to the directions under palette layout.

2. PALETTE KNIVES AND BRUSHES

    Palette knife for *mixing paint* (long blade)
    Offset knife for *painting*

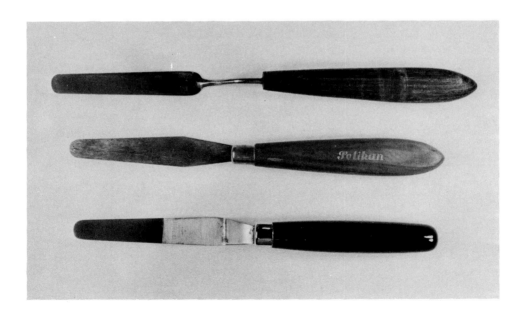

Brushes

BRISTLE-FLAT (filbert-shaped if possible)

10 or # **12** — For painting on umber wash and large areas in paintings.

2 and # **4** — For smaller details in painting, such as highlights, flowers, leaves, windows, trees, etc.

SABLE-ROUND

10 or # **8** — For sectioning canvas preparatory to drawing, and for drawing in subject.

6 — For finishing touches and extra fine details such as stems, rigging for boats, highlights, etc.

3. OIL AND KEROSENE

Poppy oil — for brush painting. It does not get gummy or yellow painting. No oil is used for palette knife painting.

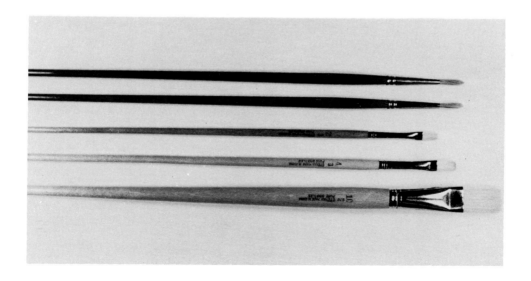

Kerosene — instead of turpentine. It is cheaper and practically odorless. It can be bought at gas stations in gallon quantities and is used in cleaning brushes, palette, fingers, etc. Kerosene is also used with burnt umber for wash for canvas.

4. OTHER MATERIALS

Large square wooden or plastic palette — some come with the box. No artistic ones, please. They are small and awkward to handle.

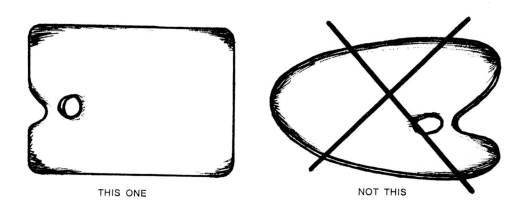

THIS ONE   NOT THIS

Metal or wooden paint box — the metal box is sturdy and will not warp.

Oil pan

Small juice can — for kerosene.

Toilet paper — no cloths. It is cleaner and disposable.

Litter bag — for soiled toilet paper.

Saran Wrap — (or wax paper or tinfoil) to preserve neat piles of paint, or paint left on palette which has been moved out of the mixing area.

Palette must be kept clean in the mixing area between painting sessions. The old paint will dry in hard ridges. If the paint does harden, pass a lighted candle over the palette to loosen the paint, and the palette can then be scraped clean.

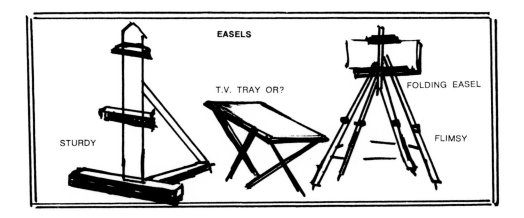

EASELS

T.V. TRAY OR?

STURDY

FOLDING EASEL

FLIMSY

5. EASEL, — **sturdy wood studio type, medium priced.** The folding kind is a horrible contraption and is constantly collapsing and, also, takes up more room.

6. CANVAS — (one of the following)

    A. **Stretch canvas** — buy already stretched until you are more experienced. A badly stretched canvas will result in ripples at the edges.

    B. **Canvas board** — excellent for beginners. Inexpensive and adequate.

    C. **Masonite** — use the rough side and cover with several coats of undercoat household white paint for painting with brush. If you are using the knife for painting, the undercoat on the masonite is not essential — use chalk for drawing. Masonite is the least expensive of all, especially for very large paintings, and the texture is very interesting. You can buy it at any lumber yard.

7. WORK AREA — the ideal would be a room with north light, etc. *Forget it*. You will most likely end up with a corner of any room that is spare, using electric light. After all, Michelangelo painted on his back for four years with a candle strapped to his head — and you can't do any better than the Sistine Chapel.

"AFTER ALL, MICHELANGELO
PAINTED ON HIS BACK..."

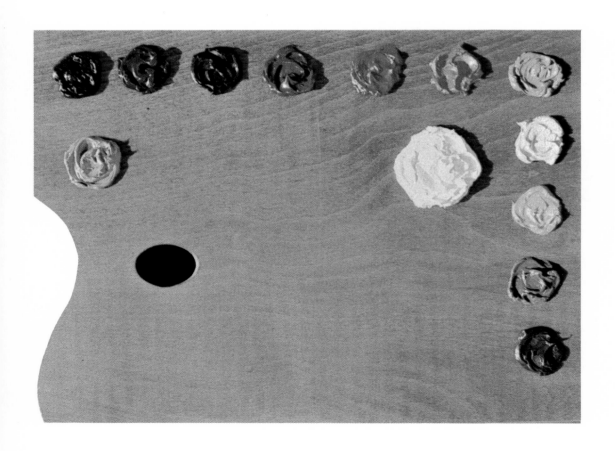

PAINTING PROCEDURES
Preparatory steps

Because you are an absolute beginner and don't know where to begin, this simplified system will get you started painting. You will learn by repetition so that the simple mechanics will become automatic — very much like learning to drive.

Read these general instructions first, so that you will become familiar with the specific instructions in the following painting exercises and the color formulas. You will notice that you only have to concentrate on one painting operation at a time.

Important: In studying palette layout, notice that **purple, mixed green,** and **aqua** are mixed *on* the palette in exact amounts as indicated on palette layout. (These colors are not on the list of painting supplies.) It is extremely essential, especially when using the following color formulas, to *match* the above *three colors,* after mixing, with the corresponding colors shown on the *color palette layout*.

1. The palette should be set up the same way each time, and a copy of the set-up kept in paint box.

2. Stain canvas with thin umber wash, always using # 10 flat bristle brush (umber and kerosene) (except masonite). Then wipe canvas dry with

PALETTE LAYOUT

BURNT UMBER

ULTRA-MARINE BLUE

PURPLE (DARK)
½ ALIZ. CRIMSON
½ ULTRA BLUE
IF MADDER LAKE
½ MORE ADDED.

ALIZARIN CRIMSON
OR MADDER LAKE

VERMILION (RED)

ORANGE

OCHRE

AQUA
1 PART THALO GREEN
2 PARTS ZINC WHITE

ZINC WHITE

NAPLES YELLOW

CAD. YELLOW MED.

2 PARTS CAD. YELLOW
1 PART THALO GREEN

MIXED GREEN

THALO GREEN

KEEP OPENING ON LEFT

ZINC YELLOW
BURNT SIENNA

ADDED FOR SPECIAL PROJECTS

tissue for warmer, richer color on stained canvas.   Remove all white.

3. Section canvas at all times with brush and kerosene and umber wash. Use chalk on masonite.

4. In placing work on canvas, start at the bottom and place marking for objects or subjects before drawing them in for correct placement and size. Use squares as guide lines — invaluable in street scenes or anything where perspective is used.   Put objects in a box.

5. Put in loose drawing with # 10 round sable brush and umber wash. Eliminate detail and stick to general form of subject matter, such as no leaves on trees or in florals, or riggings on boats, or petals on flowers, etc. No little fence posts or chimney pots.   Paint in details later.

6. Most important of all: *before mixing color or even in the planning of picture, decide where the light is coming from and loosely add lines where the shadows will be.   And continue to be conscious of light and shadow* until the last stroke is added.

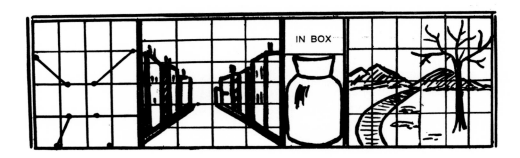

The following are the basic cool and warm colors (not counting tints derived from these colors):

WARM: *yellow, red, orange*   COOL: *blue, green, purple*

Primary colors are blue, red and yellow. You can make all other colors from these. Cool colors tend to gray or cool warm colors... and vice versa. Use the complementary or graying color sparingly. Warm colors advance (foreground); cool colors recede (background).

8

Always use knife for mixing paint. Using a brush will ruin it. Also, always put the three piles of paint out of the mixing area on the palette when through, in order to mix three piles for other objects in the picture. Do not discard. This keeps palette and paint clean and fresh. When using brush to paint, *do not rub brush in paint.* This spreads the brush and makes it too thick to give clean strokes. Just pick up paint on brush, apply to canvas and stroke it on... in the form of the object being painted. E.g., for round objects, round strokes. *Don't just fill in empty spaces.* You are creating a form; *always be conscious of form.*

Tonal Values

Each area on the canvas (background, objects, etc.) is broken down into at least *three tonal values: light, medium and dark.* As you become more experienced, two additional tones are added in polishing the painting: the brightest highlight, and accenting the shadow. In fruit, e.g., if desired, for accenting the brilliance of color, light strokes of aqua are added, usually in the shadows.

1. The medium, or mother color (the general color of object) is mixed first.
2. Divide medium color into three piles — one small (light tone), and two piles of equal size.
3. To the small or light tone, add twice as much white and nearly always a smidge of Naples yellow.
4. Do not touch middle tone.
5. To the dark or third tone, add purple or other darkening agent. (*See instructions.*) Easy does it. If original color is lost by adding too much purple or other darkening agent, add some of color used for middle (medium) color. E.g., more mixed green if painting leaves.
6. Do not add purple as a general rule to sky and water colors.

Getting Started

1. *Paint in dark tones first, then middle tones, then light tones.* Only mix tones where they meet so as not to lose tonal value or muddy color. This is very important to preserve lights and darks in the painting.
2. In the *shadows* of the painting, the *medium* and *dark* of the color are used; in the *light area*, the *medium* and *light* tones of color are used. This is of course a flexible arrangement. And, again, watch strokes — the form is the thing. But please, no spumoni — *colors must blend.* (*See paintings.*)

3. Oil or varnish is used sparingly in brush painting. Don't let it run on painting. For knife painting no oil or varnish is used.

4. Work in painting like Nature: logically. For example:

Landscape: Background or sky first. Always put light tone at horizon, then middle tone, then dark tone at the top. Then ground color, then trees and other objects last. Use large # 10 flat bristle brush for large areas, sky, background of any kind; use offset palette knife in knife painting.

Still life: Background first, then foreground, then vase or whatever. Then put flowers in vase; same for fruit, etc.

Seascape: Generally same sequence as landscape.

See breakdown of paintings for exercises and separate color charts.

WHAT SHALL I PAINT?

In order to avoid frustration or despair, the choice of subject is extremely important for the beginner. In other words: *Keep it simple.* For example, no burning desert scenes with Arabs, camels and dancing girls. Actually, original work should be attempted only after one has mastered the simple mechanics of painting. *So in order to become familiar with the procedures and color formulas, copy from the carefully chosen subjects in this manual.* Even try different color combinations with the same subjects.

Next, the aspiring painter should possibly *copy from the Impressionists.* These are best suited for the novice because of excellent color and some distortion of form, which is permissible and charming. A new student tends to paint very detailed pictures of what he knows to be there instead of what he sees. For example, there was the student who painted black blobs in the road of a street scene. She informed me they were the grease marks left by the cars. But most important: through copying you are being conditioned to "see" painting professionally right from the beginning. In other words, you are in effect an apprentice (practiced by the old masters in learning). It is only after you have mastered the basic techniques of painting and composition that you can be discriminating in your choice of subject.

The Impressionist generation consisted of Monet, Degas, Pizzaro, Manet, Cezanne, etc. On the other hand, you can use instead photographic color reproductions of simple compositions. You can find them at any art store. These can be a marvellous aid to a beginner. As a matter of fact, *Manet, Degas* (who copied from the masters and evolved his own style), *and Lautrec used photos for their paintings; and the best work of Utrillo was done exclusively from picture post cards.*

At the beginning you need all the help you can get, and remember: in art, the end result justifies the means. For, contrary to what is commonly believed, copying doesn't necessarily mean you imitate the artist's style. No two painters see things exactly alike unless it's deliberate. It takes experience to be a copyist.

COLOR FORMULAS FOR PAINTINGS

In a painting, color is most important, even more than the drawing.
At the risk of sounding unartistic and homey, I have broken down color into almost exact amounts, rather like a recipe. (No, this is not a cooking class.) I'm going to use *spoons* for measuring. This helps to keep amounts uniform and I assume everyone is already quite familiar with spoons. Of course, this gives me qualms as I have visions of paint actually being measured out with spoons. Don't — just eyeball it! This naturally means *the amounts are not level.*
This is the table of amounts used in color mixtures.

TABLE OF MEASUREMENTS

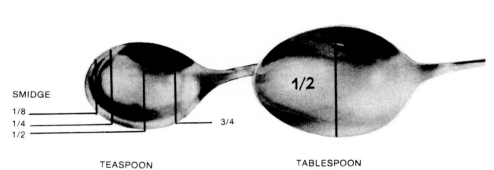

SMIDGE
1/8
1/4
1/2
3/4
1/2

TEASPOON

TABLESPOON

These amounts are geared mostly for knife painting, which requires more paint, but they can also be used for brush painting. However, for now paint with the palette knife. It's a bit awkward at first but best for a beginner since it almost never results in a dull, smudgy painting. It's also easier to retain brilliant clean tonal values with the palette knife.
The following color combinations are a boon to beginners because they take the guesswork out of mixing color. And if you follow carefully the formula for each color mixed, you will always get the correct tonal values.
For example: if you want to paint a *sky*, turn to the *chart for a sky;* if you want to paint *yellow flowers*, consult *chart for mixture of tones of yellow*. Then follow directions.
As you become more experienced you will want to improvise and go on from the original three tonal values of light, medium and dark.
These color formulas are a means to an end — not ends in themselves.
But it is most important now to follow directions carefully, and to learn by repetition.

Painting Guides

1. *Easy does it* when mixing color.   You can always add more.   Keep tonal values.

2. The colors may look unrelated after mixing and a little dull on the palette; this is normal.   When applied on canvas in a composition they not only make sense.   They also *make a painting*.

3. Test the colors on a canvas after mixing.   Just a patch is enough.

At this point you are saying impatiently, "But when do I paint??" If you follow and learn these simple directions first, you will save time and aggravation in the long run.   And in the mixing of color, you will *make your mistakes* and experiments *on the palette* and *not on the painting*.

CHART FOR BASIC COLORS

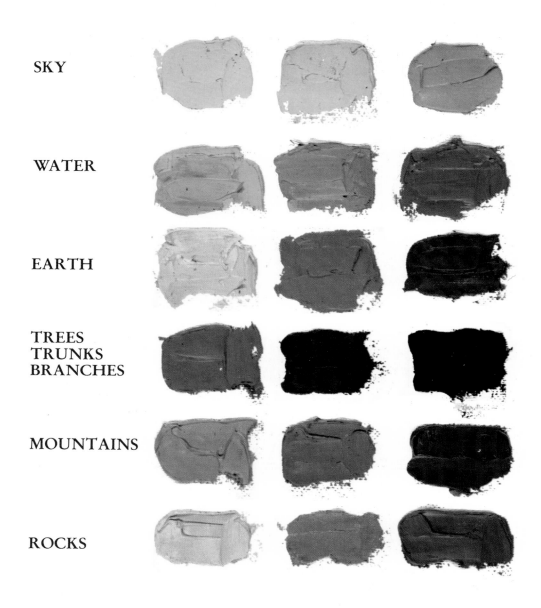

SKY

WATER

EARTH

TREES
TRUNKS
BRANCHES

MOUNTAINS

ROCKS

The above three tonal values of each.

Basic color combinations

Note:

1. *Mix the following colors as directed with the straight knife. Keep knife clean in going from one color tone to another.*

2. *Again, there should be a distinct difference in the tonal values of light, medium and dark for each color combination.*

3. *Remember: we always mix the medium, or " mother," color first. This is the general color of object. Then mix a " light " and a " dark " tonal value of that color. Also, color will look unrelated on palette.*

4. *Mix in the order given.*

SKY

Medium or Mother Color

>**1 tablespoon zinc white**
>
>**3/4 teaspoon aqua**
>
>**1/4 teaspoon ultramarine blue**
>
>**1/8 teaspoon orange** (warm color, graying agent)
>(easy does it)

Mix and then separate color into three parts. Small part will be light tone and two piles of equal size will be used for the medium tone (you do not touch) and the dark tone.

1. SMALL PART — 3/4 teaspoon — will be light tone.

   Add: **1 teaspoon zinc white**

   >**1/4 teaspoon Naples yellow** (color will be greenish)

2. SECOND PART — for medium tone. *Do not touch.*

3. THIRD PART — for dark tone.

   Add: **1/4 teaspoon ultramarine blue**

   >**1/2 teaspoon aqua**
   >
   >**1/4 teaspoon orange.** Go easy on the orange to avoid graying.

WATER, SEA, ETC.

Same mixture as sky with one exception:

Add **1/2 teaspoon mixed green** to the first mixture (medium tone) to give the water — a reflection of the sky — a greenish cast, and a light tone near shore, which is shallow and therefore yellow-green.

EARTH

Medium Color

> **1 teaspoon yellow ochre**
> **1/2 teaspoon zinc white**
> **1/8 teaspoon burnt sienna**

Mix and separate color into three parts — one small part for the light tone and two piles of equal size.

1. SMALL PART — 1/2 teaspoon — for the light tone.

   Add: **1 teaspoon white**
   1/2 teaspoon Naples yellow

2. SECOND PART — for medium tone. As usual, *do not touch.*

3. THIRD PART — for dark tone.

   Add: **1/4 teaspoon purple**
   Smidge of mixed green
   (on palette — easy does it)

TREES — Foliage covered in mixtures of green (*see chart, page 14*). If you have a "forest," double the measurements of the following.

Medium Color

> **3/4 teaspoon burnt umber**
> **1/2 teaspoon yellow ochre**
> **1/4 teaspoon alizarin crimson or madder lake**
> **1/4 teaspoon orange**

Mix and separate into three parts — one small for the light tone and two parts of equal size.

1. SMALL PART — 1/2 teaspoon — for the light tone.

    Add: **1/2 teaspoon zinc white**
    1/4 teaspoon Naples yellow
    Smidge of orange (consult table of measurements)

2. SECOND PART — for medium tone. As usual, *do not touch*.

3. THIRD PART — for dark tone.

    Add: **1/2 teaspoon purple**
    1/4 teaspoon orange

MOUNTAINS — Let's assume for now that most mountains are purple tones.

Medium Color

    1 teaspoon white
    1/2 teaspoon purple
    1/4 teaspoon yellow ochre
    1/4 teaspoon mixed green

Mix and separate color into three parts — one small for the light tone and two parts of equal size.

1. SMALL PART — 1/2 teaspoon — will be light tone.

    Add: **1/2 teaspoon white**
    1/4 teaspoon Naples yellow
    1/4 teaspoon orange

2. SECOND PART — for medium tone. As usual, *do not touch*.

3. THIRD PART — for dark tone.

    Add: **1/2 teaspoon purple**
    1/4 teaspoon blue
    1/2 teaspoon orange
    1/4 teaspoon yellow ochre

ROCKS

Medium Color

> **1 teaspoon white**
> **3/4 teaspoon ochre**
> **1/2 teaspoon purple**
> **Smidge of orange**

Mix and separate into three parts — one small for the light tone and two parts of equal size.

1. SMALL PART — 1/2 teaspoon — for the light tone.

   Add: **1/2 teaspoon zinc white**
   1/4 teaspoon Naples yellow
   Smidge of orange

2. SECOND PART — for medium tone. As usual, *do not touch*.

3. THIRD PART — for dark tone.

   Add: **1/2 teaspoon purple**
   Smidge of orange

CHART FOR MIXTURES OF COLOR TONES

RED

WHITE

BLUE

PURPLE

ORANGE

YELLOW

GREEN

BLACK

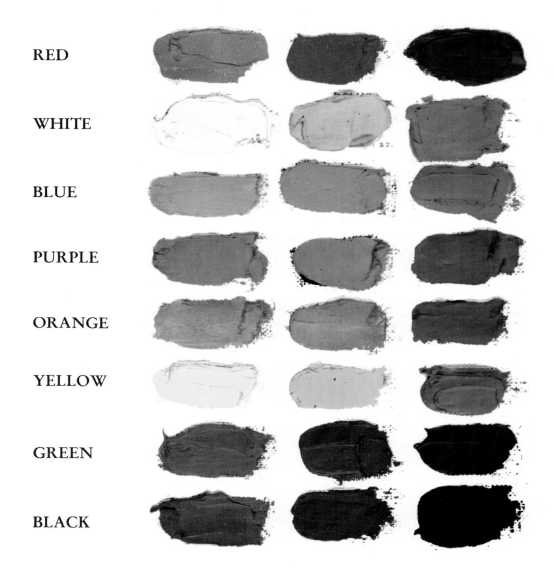

Mixtures of color tones

Important: If in darkening third part of any color you lose some original color, add color needed using the same as used in original mixture. For example, in the mixture of green where the third part is darkened with purple, if it looks no longer somewhat green, pick up about 1/8 teaspoon of mixed green to restore color. But keep dark green tonal value intact.

Mix in order given and keep palette layout handy.

RED

Medium Tone

> **1 1/4 teaspoons vermilion only**

Separate vermilion into three parts — one small for the light tone and two parts of equal size.

1. SMALL PART — 1/2 teaspoon — to be light tone.

     Add: **1/4 teaspoon orange**
     1/2 teaspoon white
     1/4 teaspoon vermilion

2. SECOND PART — for medium tone. *Do not touch.*

3. THIRD PART — for dark tone.

     Add: **1/2 teaspoon madder lake or alizarin crimson**

WHITE — To be used for clouds, sea foam, snow, flowers, vases, vegetables, etc.
Note: Tones of white are one of the few colors to be mixed a little differently.

Light Tone

> **1 1/2 teaspoons white**
> **1/8 teaspoon Naples yellow** (easy does it)

Mix and separate into three *equal* piles.

1. FIRST PART — for light tone. *Do not touch.*

2. SECOND PART — for medium tone.

     Add: **1/8 teaspoon burnt umber** (will look beige)
     Smidge of aqua

3. THIRD PART — for dark tone.

Add: **1/4 teaspoon burnt umber**
1/8 teaspoon aqua
Smidge of orange (will look dark)

BLUE — To be used for flowers, clothing, vases, etc.

Medium Tone

1 teaspoon zinc white
1/4 teaspoon ultramarine blue
1/2 teaspoon aqua
1/4 teaspoon orange

Mix and separate into three parts — one small for the light tone and two parts of equal size.

1. SMALL PART — 1/2 teaspoon — for light tone.

Add: **1/2 teaspoon zinc white**
Tiny smidge of Naples yellow

2. SECOND PART — for medium tone. *Do not touch.*

3. THIRD PART — for dark tone.

Add: **1/4 teaspoon blue**
1/4 teaspoon aqua
1/8 teaspoon orange

PURPLE — To be used for fruits, vegetables, flowers, etc.

Medium Tone

1 teaspoon white
1/2 teaspoon purple
Smidge of yellow ochre (easy)

Mix and separate into three parts — one small for the light tone and two parts of equal size.

1. SMALL PART — 1/2 teaspoon — for light tone.

Add: **1/2 teaspoon white**
Smidge of Naples yellow

2. SECOND PART — for medium tone. *Do not touch.*

3. THIRD PART — for dark tone.

   Add: **1/4 teaspoon purple**
   Tiny smidge of yellow ochre and orange

ORANGE — To be used for fruits, vegetables, flowers, clothing, etc.

Medium Tone

   1 1/2 teaspoons orange only

Separate orange into three parts — one small for the light tone and two parts of equal size.

1. SMALL PART — 1/2 teaspoon — for light tone.

   Add: **1/2 teaspoon white**
   1/4 teaspoon cadmium yellow medium

2. SECOND PART — for medium tone. *Do not touch.*

3. THIRD PART — for dark tone.

   Add: **1/2 teaspoon madder lake or alizarin crimson**

YELLOW — To be used for fruits, vegetables, flowers, etc.
   Note: Zinc yellow is used in this mixture. This color is mixed differently.

Medium Tone

   1 1/4 teaspoons cadmium yellow medium

Separate it into two piles of equal size.

1. ONE PART — for medium tone. *Do not touch.*

2. SECOND PART — for dark tone.

   Add: **1/2 teaspoon yellow ochre**

Light Tone (separate mixture)

   1/2 teaspoon white
   1/2 teaspoon zinc yellow

GREEN — To be used for vegetables, grass, trees, shrubs (vegetation), florals, leaves, etc.

Medium Tone

> **1 teaspoon yellow ochre**
> **1 teaspoon mixed green**
> **1/8 teaspoon vermilion** (easy does it)

Mix and separate into three piles — one small for light tone and two parts of equal size.

1. SMALL PART — 1/2 teaspoon — for light tone.

   Add: **1/2 teaspoon zinc white**
   1/2 teaspoon cadmium yellow medium

2. SECOND PART — for medium tone. *Do not touch.*

3. THIRD PART — for dark tone.

   Add: **1/2 teaspoon purple**
   1/2 teaspoon mixed green (easy)

BLACK — Rarely used except for accents, lamps, fences, vases, clothing and anything where black tones are needed. Also mixed differently.

Dark Tone (mixed first)

> **1/2 teaspoon burnt umber**
> **1/2 teaspoon ultramarine blue**

Separate into three parts — one small for the light tone and two parts of equal size.

1. SMALL PART — 1/4 teaspoon — for light tone.

   Add: **1/2 teaspoon white**
   Tiny smidge of Naples yellow and orange

2. SECOND PART — for medium tone.

   Add: **1/4 teaspoon white**
   Smidge of orange

3. THIRD PART — for dark tone. *Do not touch.*

CHART FOR BACKGROUND COLOR COMBINATIONS

FLORALS - HOUSES - BOATS etc.

BURNT ORANGE

LIGHT GREEN

DARK GREEN

YELLOW OCHRE

Background color combinations

1. *These mixed grayed colors can be used in other objects of paintings and are interchangeable.*
2. *Mix amounts in the order given.*
3. *If you have a larger canvas and need more background, mix another half batch — or double the measurements.*
4. *If unsure of colors check palette sheet. Keep knife clean in going from one tone to another.*

BURNT ORANGE

Medium Color

> **1 3/4 teaspoons orange**
> **1/4 teaspoon madder lake or alizarin crimson**

Mix and separate into three parts — one small part for the light tone and two parts of equal size.

1. SMALL PART — 3/4 teaspoon — for the light tone.
   Add: **1/2 teaspoon zinc white**
   1/4 teaspoon cadmium yellow medium
2. SECOND PART — for medium tone. *Do not touch.*
3. THIRD PART — for dark tone.
   Add: **1/2 teaspoon madder lake or alizarin crimson**

YELLOW OCHRE

Medium Color

> **1 tablespoon yellow ochre only**

Separate color into three parts — one small part for the light tone and two parts of equal size.

1. SMALL PART — 1/2 teaspoon — for the light tone.
   Add: **3/4 teaspoon white**
2. SECOND PART — for medium tone. *Do not touch.*
3. THIRD PART — for dark tone.
   Add: **1/2 teaspoon purple**

LIGHT GREEN

Medium Color

> **1 tablespoon zinc white**
> **1 teaspoon yellow ochre**
> **1/2 teaspoon mixed green**
> **1/8 teaspoon vermilion**

Mix and separate into three parts — one small part for the light tone and two parts of equal size.

1. SMALL PART — 3/4 teaspoon — will be light tone.
   Add: **3/4 teaspoon zinc white**

2. SECOND PART — for medium tone. *Do not touch.*

3. THIRD PART — for dark tone.

   Add: **1/4 teaspoon purple**
   1/8 teaspoon mixed thalo green

DARK GREEN

Medium Tone

> **1 tablespoon yellow ochre**
> **1/2 teaspoon mixed green**
> **1/2 teaspoon purple**

Mix and separate into three parts — one small for the light tone and two parts of equal size.

1. SMALL PART — 3/4 teaspoon — will be light tone.
   Add: **3/4 teaspoon white**

2. SECOND PART — for medium tone. *Do not touch.*

3. THIRD PART — for dark tone.

   Add: **1/2 teaspoon purple**
   1/4 teaspoon pure thalo green (unmixed from palette)
   1/4 teaspoon ochre

CHART FOR COLOR TINTS

YELLOW TINT

ORANGE TINT

RED TINT

PURPLE TINT

BLUE TINT

GREEN TINT

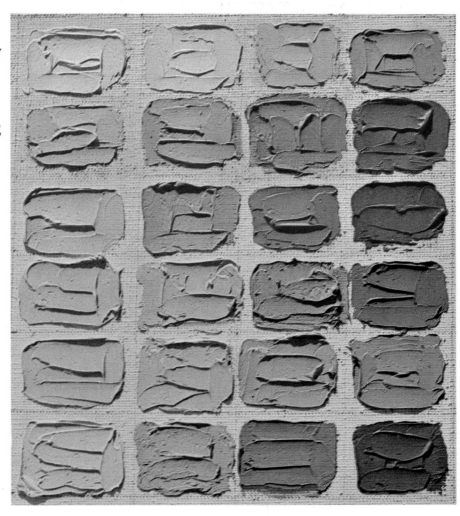

EXTRA-LIGHT   **LIGHT**   **MEDIUM**   **DARK**

COLOR TINTS

1. *These color tints are invaluable in painting, especially for florals, but they can be used in any painting where pastel shades are required.*
2. *When mixing colors for tints: easy does it. You can always add more color.*
3. *Keep knife clean in going from one tone to another.*

YELLOW TINT

Medium tone

> **1 1/4 teaspoons zinc white**
> **1/2 teaspoon cadmium yellow medium**
> **1/4 teaspoon zinc yellow**

Mix and separate into three parts — one small part for the light tone and two parts of equal size.

1. SMALL PART — 1/2 teaspoon — for light tone.

    Add: **1 teaspoon zinc white**
    1/4 teaspoon zinc yellow

2. SECOND PART — for medium tone. *Do not touch.*

3. THIRD PART — for dark tone.

    Add: **3/4 teaspoon cadmium yellow medium**
    1/2 teaspoon yellow ochre
    1/4 teaspoon orange

4. FOURTH PART — 1/4 teaspoon light tone — extra-light tone.

    Add: **3/4 teaspoon zinc white**

ORANGE TINT

Medium tone

> **1 teaspoon zinc white**
> **1/2 teaspoon orange**
> **1/4 teaspoon cadmium yellow**

Mix and separate color into three parts — one small part for the light tone and two parts of equal size.

1. SMALL PART — 1/3 teaspoon — for light tone.

Add: **3/4 teaspoon zinc white**
1/8 teaspoon cadmium yellow

2. SECOND PART — for medium tone. *Do not touch.*

3. THIRD PART — for dark tone.

Add: **3/4 teaspoon orange**
1/8 teaspoon vermilion

4. FOURTH PART — 1/4 teaspoon light tone — for extra-light tone.

Add: **3/4 teaspoon zinc white**

RED TINT

Medium tone

1 1/4 tablespoons zinc white
1/2 teaspoon vermilion
1/4 teaspoon orange

Mix and separate color into three parts — one small part for the light tone and two parts of equal size.

1. SMALL PART — 1/2 teaspoon — for light tone.

Add: **1 1/4 teaspoons zinc white**
Smidge of Naples yellow
Smidge of orange

2. SECOND PART — for medium tone. *Do not touch.*

3. THIRD PART — for dark tone.

Add: **3/4 teaspoon vermilion**
1/8 teaspoon orange

4. FOURTH PART — 1/4 teaspoon light tone — for extra-light tone.

Add: **3/4 teaspoon zinc white**

PURPLE TINT — *Note:* For a cooler or bluer purple tint, eliminate madder lake.

Medium tone

> **1 1/2 teaspoons zinc white**
> **1/2 teaspoon purple**
> **1/2 teaspoon madder lake**

Mix and separate color into three parts — one small part for the light tone and two parts of equal size.

1. SMALL PART — 1/2 teaspoon — for light tone.

   Add: **1 1/4 teaspoons zinc white**
   Smidge of madder lake

2. SECOND PART — for medium tone. *Do not touch.*

3. THIRD PART — for dark tone.

   Add: **1/2 teaspoon purple**
   1/4 teaspoon madder lake

4. FOURTH PART — 1/4 teaspoon light tone — for extra-light tone.

   Add: **3/4 teaspoon zinc white**

BLUE TINT

Medium tone

> **1 1/4 tablespoons zinc white**
> **1/4 teaspoon aqua**
> **1/8 teaspoon blue**

Mix and separate color into three parts — one small part for the light tone and two parts of equal size.

1. SMALL PART — 1/2 teaspoon — for light tone.

   Add: **1 teaspoon zinc white**
   1/8 teaspoon aqua

2. SECOND PART — for medium tone. *Do not touch.*

3. THIRD PART — for dark tone.

   Add: **1/4 teaspoon blue**
   1/2 teaspoon aqua

4. FOURTH PART — 1/4 teaspoon light tone — for extra-light tone.

    Add: **3/4 teaspoon zinc white**

GREEN TINT

Medium tone

> **1/2 teaspoon yellow ochre**
> **1/2 teaspoon mixed green**
> **1 teaspoon zinc white**
> **Smidge of cadmium yellow**

Mix and separate color into three parts — one small part for the light tone and two parts of equal size.

1. SMALL PART — 1/2 teaspoon — for light tone.

    Add: **1 teaspoon zinc white**
           1/4 teaspoon cadmium yellow

2. SECOND PART — for medium tone. *Do not touch.*

3. THIRD PART — for dark tone.

    Add: **1/2 teaspoon mixed green**
        Smidge of purple
        Smidge of cadmium yellow

4. FOURTH PART — 1/4 teaspoon light tone — for extra-light tone.

    Add: **3/4 teaspoon zinc white**

ARRANGING YOUR WORK AREA

Note:

1. *You should not paint more than three hours at one time.*

2. *Do not set up complete palette until drawing is finished. Just squeeze out 1/2 teaspoon burnt umber for wash and drawing.*

3. *Clean mixing area, and remove loose paint. To preserve color left on palette, cover well with Saran Wrap, wax paper, tinfoil or whatever.*

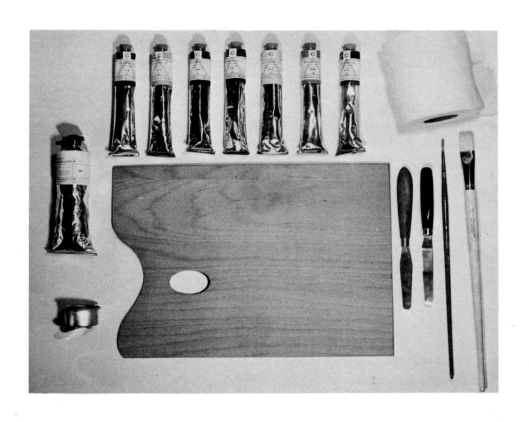

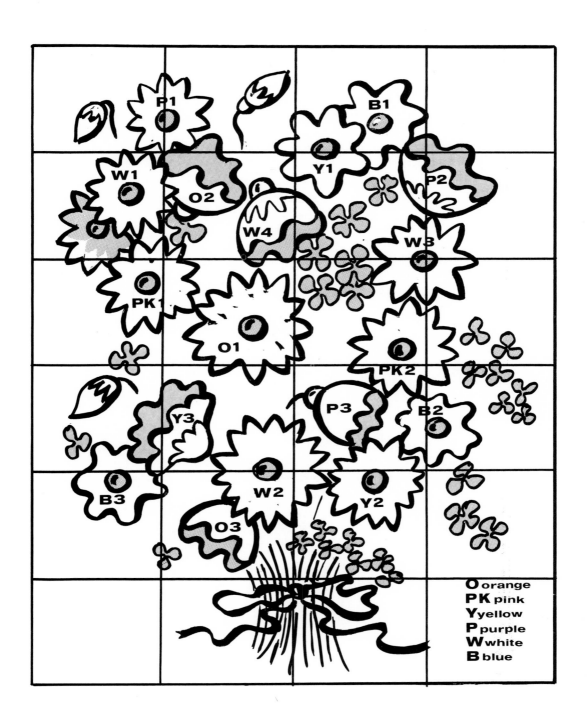

O orange
PK pink
Y yellow
P purple
W white
B blue

LESSON ONE
FLORAL STILL LIFE ARRANGEMENT

Session I

Still Life (usually fruit or flowers):

Still life is best for a beginner. It is less demanding and can be an excellent "warm up" project if one hasn't painted in a while. Getting started is like that first dip in an icy sea. So plunge right in — you'll soon get used to it and love it.

This wild, gay, spring bouquet was painted to *utilize all* the *colors* of the *Chart for Color Tints.* (*See color plate, page 27.*) Since the amounts of mixed colors are more than adequate, you can paint other florals. For example, small florals using only one color for the flowers. (*See exercises following.*)

The Drawing

A. THE WASH AND SECTIONING

1. Your canvas (16″ × 20″, or approximate size) is placed firmly on your easel. You are wearing old clothes or a smock. You have adequate light. It's a good idea to clamp a small lamp to the top of the easel if you can't get sufficient light. On your right your work table or TV tray is laid out in orderly fashion. (What's said about artists being messy is not always true.)

2. *Squeeze* out **1/2 teaspoon of burnt umber.**

3. Pick up your large **# 10 flat bristle brush;** dip it partly into the kerosene (it should not be dripping), and then into the burnt umber on the palette, pulling some aside to make a light wash. The wash should be rather thin. Apply to canvas, covering with wash. Don't make it too dark or runny. (This same procedure is used for all oil canvases.) Here the stroke does not matter. Wipe excess moisture with tissue but leave damp. That is so you can easily wipe out mistakes with tissue in the drawing, which is done with the same umber wash.

4. Pick up **# 8 or # 10 round sable brush** and section off canvas with same umber wash, again not too dark or runny. *We do not use pencil or charcoal for drawing.* They are difficult to change, dirty the paint and create an inhibited drawing. Section the canvas with five evenly spaced horizontal lines and four vertical lines. A floral is usually vertical.

5. Next put in the simple drawing (reduced to simple form), again with the same umber wash and the # 8 or # 10 round sable brush. Use tissue to erase if necessary.

36

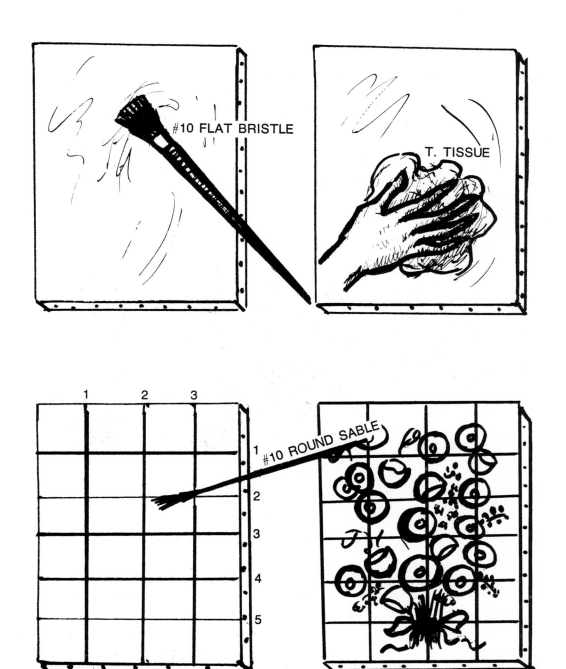

B. THE FLOWERS

1. Observe flowers in completed drawing on page 35 and place circles as you see them. Start from center of floral and work outwards. The flowers in the center are larger. The ones on the outside of the bouquet are smaller.

2. Shape circle according to the angles and types of flowers. This floral contains mostly daisy-type flowers, poppies and other small flowers. (*Important: the small flowers are not drawn in. They are painted in last, between the flowers.*)

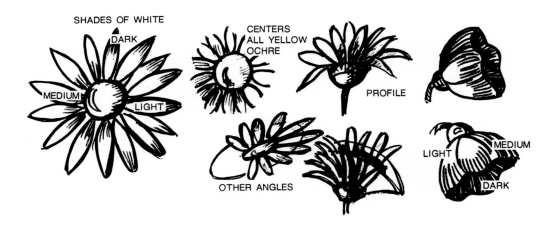

3. Nearly always place a small circle in the middle of flowers (except those in profile).

4. Do not draw in leaves, stems, and petals. These, along with the blue and white small flowers, are worked out with tonal values of paint. So don't panic.

5. *Most important: after drawing, decide where the light is coming from, and be conscious of light and shadow until the last stroke is added.* The light in this painting is coming from the left.

The drawing is finished.

Now, let's paint

The Background

1. Set up your complete palette. See palette layout, page 7. Don't squeeze burnt sienna for now, however, and add zinc yellow. Put out enough paint — about the size of circles on palette. Use straight knife for mixing. *Important: do not cover any given area with one color and then try to put another color over it.* Put tonal values in the indicated areas where they belong.

2. The background colors will be mixed first. Consult *Chart* for *Background Color Combinations* for "tones of dark green." (*See color plate, page 24.*)

3. *Mix background color* (light, medium, and dark) *with* **straight knife.** Easy does it; you can always add a little more color. Maintain distinct tonal values. Clean knife.

4. Mentally divide the canvas *vertically* in *thirds* before applying the *light, medium, and dark* for the *background colors.*

5. Pick up **offset knife** and scoop up a little of the **dark tone.** Nearly always start with the dark tone. *Do not load the knife with paint.*

6. Paint in the dark tone on the right side of canvas with long sweeping strokes (hold knife lightly and do not cover flowers) until a third is covered. *Clean knife with* **tissue.**

7. Scoop up some **medium tone,** and lightly, with the same sweeping downward strokes, cover the *second third of canvas. Blend the two tonal values only where they meet.* Go around and into the circle of flowers a little, as the petals should overlap onto the background. Clean knife.

8. Scoop up some **light tone** of the dark green and again with same stroke fill in the remaining *third of canvas.* Blend the areas of color *only* where they meet. *Do not destroy tonal values or lose flowers.*

Note: If you should run out of paint, mix another half batch to finish background. When the background is finished remove any remaining paint to just below the piles of paint on palette. (*You may need this paint to patch any spots left undone.*) Clean mixing area. You will now go on to mixing paint for the flowers. *Clean knife.* Also *put the painting aside for a few days.* It's best to work in *three-hour sessions.* The background should dry somewhat for easier application of flowers.

Session II

Flowers

1. Because this is a multicolor floral, it's logical when you mix one of the colors to *paint all flowers in that color.* Hence, study individual drawings of flowers of each color, showing *designated areas of light, medium and dark tones.* (The extra-light tone is added last.)

Note: A tablet of plain or canvas paper to practice painting a few flowers, leaves, etc., before going to canvas would be a tremendous help.

2. ORANGE FLOWERS

    Begin with the orange flowers in the center. *Important: study* the *painting* on page 34, and the *completed drawing* on page 35. (The individual drawings and the completed drawings are *numbered* and *labeled* to *facilitate painting the right flowers,* in the *right place.*)
    Consult *Chart for Color Tints,* page 27, for tones of orange and mix with straight knife according to directions. Clean knife.

    A. *Daisy-type Flower No. 1:* be sure the petals of all such flowers are painted straight out from the center as shown in drawing. *Do not curve petals like a pinwheel.*

Note: The flower drawings are *precise* so you can understand the *structure* and *color areas.* The *painting,* you will notice, is much more *impressionistic.* Try for a looser painting. It's more important to retain *tonal value* than *form.*

(1) Scoop up **medium tone of orange tint** with offset knife and paint upper petals where indicated, leaving flower tips free. Try not to "draw" petals; try to paint each petal with *one stroke, easily* and *freely.* Clean knife.

(2) Scoop **light tone of orange tint** and paint the lower petals. (It will be a bit awkward at first.) Clean knife.

(3) Scoop up **dark tone of orange tint** and paint tips of upper petals, *blending slightly* with a clean knife. Do not lose *tonal value.* (Put a few touches of pure vermilion on upper petals.)

(4) Scoop up the extra-light tone and lightly tip the lower three petals as indicated in drawing. Clean knife.

(5) Paint in **yellow ochre** center with *round strokes,* overlapping petals a little. Center should be large and round. You are *creating a form, not filling in an empty space.* (*See drawing page 38.*) Apply curved highlight of **Naples yellow** (colors unmixed from palette). Clean knife.

Note: All centers shown in flowers are painted the *same way* and *same color.*

(6) Scoop up *very little* **purple.** *Lightly* and *thinly go around center* on right side and between several petals. (*See painting page 34.*) This means the center is raised. You will notice all centers are out-lined the same way for depth.
No. 1 flower is finished. Clean knife.

B. *Orange Poppy No. 2: Three tonal values*
(1) Scoop up the **dark tone of orange tint** and paint in top of poppy to the curved line, using a *fanlike stroke,* following the shape of the flower. Clean knife.

(2) Scoop up **medium tone** and paint the bottom half of poppy with the same *fanlike stroke.* Clean knife.

(3) Scoop up **light tone** and paint three petal-like blobs (as shown in drawing) over **medium tone.** Blend lightly where tones meet. Clean knife.

C. *Orange Poppy No. 3*

(1) Scoop up **dark tone of orange tint** and paint the *lower part* of poppy to *curved line*. Clean knife.

(2) Scoop up **medium tone** and paint right side of poppy *only* as shown. Watch strokes. Clean knife.

(3) Scoop up **light tone of orange tint** and, using a curved stroke, paint remaining area on poppy. Blend lightly; do not lose tonal values. Accent the wavy line on both poppies between tones with pure vermilion. (*See painting page 34.*) This will give flowers a little jazz.

(4) Pick up a little **extra-light tone** and put a blob, as shown, on *center petal only*. This is the "highlight."
The orange flowers are finished. Clean knife.

Note: Remove any remaining individual piles of orange tint paint to a sheet of tin foil or a foil pie tin. Keep each pile intact and when foil is filled with paint of all colors, cover lightly with foil and keep in a *cool* place. *Save for floral exercises.* Clean mixing area for another color.

Since the same flowers are repeated in all colors (with the exception of small blue and white flowers), study the drawings of each and follow the same directions used for painting of orange flowers.

3. PINK FLOWERS

Study carefully these drawings and completed drawing of floral, page 35. Study painting, page 34.

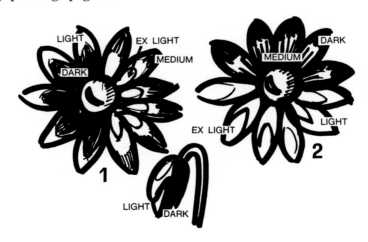

A. Consult *Chart for Color Tints for tones of red.*   Mix according to directions.
B. Paint pink flowers using same directions used for daisy-type orange flowers.   (Pink flowers should be easier.)   When finished preserve color. Clean mixing area and knife.

4. YELLOW FLOWERS

Study drawings carefully.   Be sure to check numbers on both drawings, page 35 and below.   Study painting, page 34.

A. Consult *Chart for Color Tints for tones of yellow.*
B. With straight knife mix according to directions.
C. Paint flowers with offset knife as usual.
D. Put a wavy line of **pure vermilion** between light and medium color of poppy, and some on petals of No. 2 daisy (dark area).   When finished, preserve paint.   Clean mixing area and knife.

5. PURPLE FLOWERS

Study drawings carefully.   Observe painting on page 34.

1   2   3

A.   Consult *Chart for Color Tints for tones of purple*.   Mix according to directions.

B.   With offset knife loosely paint flowers according to previous directions.
Note: When poppies are finished, paint a wavy line of straight purple between dark and medium areas.   (*See painting page 34.*)

C.   Preserve leftover paint and clean mixing area and knife.

6. WHITE FLOWERS

Study drawings carefully.   Observe painting on page 34.

A.   Consult *Chart for Mixtures of Color Tones* on page 19 for **tone of white.**
White is *not* on *Chart for Color Tints*.

Note: There is an extra daisy (No. 3) not shown on drawing opposite which is painted like No. 2.

B.   Daisies No. 1 are **three tones of white.**
Daisies No. 2 and No. 3 are **medium and light tone** only.
The poppy (No. 4) is **medium and light tones with a purple wavy line between tones.**   Also, there are small dots of **purple** and **cadmium yellow** along purple line (stamens).   See painting.

C. Small white flowers will be added last. By now, the knife doesn't feel so much like a trowel and is getting easier to use. After painting white flowers, preserve paint or move it aside for small flowers. Clean mixing area and knife.

7. BLUE FLOWERS

Study drawings carefully. Note especially the small blue flowers. Study painting.

A. Consult *Chart for Color Tints for tones of blue.* Mix with straight knife according to directions.

B. The *blue daisies* are painted like the previous daisies.

C. The *small blue and white flowers* are painted the same. Use the **dark tone at the top** and the **light tone on the two lower petals of each little flower.** The flowers should be few and indefinite and should be staggered along the stem, but not in a perfect row. (*See painting page 34.*) There is one blue grouping between the other flowers and others scattered on the outside of bouquet between flowers, leaves, etc.

Note: The flowers are finished. They may look somewhat mechanical at first, but as you keep painting your paintings will look more relaxed, when you are.

8. After flowers are painted, stroke in **straight purple** — from palette where it
    looks very dark — in center between flowers. Do not load knife with
    paint. This purple — not too much, now — gives bouquet depth and
    dramatic impact.   It will look strange, but don't get hysterical as the leaves
    are painted over the purple.   Clean mixing area and knife. (*See completed
    drawing, page 35.*)

Session III

Leaves and Stems

1. LEAVES

    A. After reading these directions for painting leaves, try a few on paper until you get the feeling and proper color. Consult *Chart for Mixtures of Color Tones* for **green** and with a straight knife mix green according to directions. After green colors are mixed, look again. Think of your light and shadow. As in the flowers, you have a " dark " side and a " light " side. For the leaves on the right, or " dark " side, use **medium and dark tones of green;** for leaves on the left, **medium and light tones of green.**

    B. Unless it is a very distinctive leaf (e.g., a calla lily leaf), we paint in just a suggestion of leaves. The leaves are used merely as a background or a prop for the flowers, which are the main object in the painting. In other words, *you can just about use the same* SUGGESTION *of leaves in practically all florals.*

C. Take your offset knife and scoop up a little **dark green** color. (It's best to run the flat of your knife lightly through paint and have just a thin coating of paint the length of your knife.) *You want just a few light, delicate leaves* (easy does it — no spinach). (*See page* 47.) Press the knife down on canvas in a kind of leaf in the dark side between flowers on the outside (above). Clean knife.

D. Pick up **medium tone** and again press down color on *left side of same leaf*, as shown. Clean knife.

E. Next, in the same manner, pick up **medium tone** and go on to light side, between flowers, on the outside, and press down lightly and delicately on the top side of leaf. Clean knife.

F. Pick up **light tone** and again put in on side or edge of medium tone of same leaf, loosely, as shown.

G. On the profile of the flowers put a small pod of **dark and light tones,** as shown: first **dark,** then a small blob of **light** tone for highlight.

H. On the purple between flowers in the middle of the bouquet, press down with **dark and light green,** creating an impression of leaves. It is not necessary to cover purple completely to give this impression of foliage around flower. Do not "draw" leaves.

2. STEMS

A. There is a grouping, four inches wide, of flower stems in the middle of the bottom of the canvas. (*See drawing, page 35.*)

B. Scoop up **dark green** (mixed for leaves) and paint in half of the stems — on the *right or dark side*. Clean knife.

C. Scoop up **light tone of green** and paint in the other half of stems — *on the left or light side. Run some* **straight purple** *under flowers down all stems for about 1 1/2 inches* (shadow of flowers). *Soften stems under flowers* with suggestions of *delicate light leaves.*

D. When floral is finished take your clean knife and *lightly scratch stems* with *point of knife*, logically from your flowers toward the center and into the stems at the bottom. Do this only when you can see stems. Also, paint stems on buds **light green.**

E. Finally, the bow is painted in two shades of blue (of flowers). First, loosely paint in the light tone, then the dark tone, as indicated. Study painting, page 34. Keep it slender and graceful — do not paint a tight, heavy bow.

Now stop. **The painting is finished!** Don't keep playing with it and fretting over it.   One of the most difficult lessons you will learn in painting is KNOWING WHEN TO STOP.

At this point, you could argue that *Albert P. Ryder*, famous American painter ("Death on a Pale Horse"), in the solitude of his New York tenement, *reworked his paintings for thirty years.*   Painting over dust and grime gave a molten, jewel-like quality to his paintings.

Fine, but since it's quite possible you may *not* be another *Albert P. Ryder*, forget it.   In overworking, not only will your painting *lose* its *spontaneity and freshness*, but you *may very well lose the painting.*

"LEAVE IT ALONE!"

FLORAL COMBINATIONS EXERCISE

Because there are several different kinds of flowers in "Spring Bouquet," and you have leftover color tints, you can have fun *mix-matching flowers* and *colors*. You can also consult *Charts for Background Color Combinations* and *Mixtures of Color Tones*, if needed. Use small 9″ × 12″ canvases — they are charming. Try the few following exercises or make up your own.

1. A. Background — yellow ochre (backgrounds)
   B. Flowers — tones of white

2. A. Background — light green (backgrounds)
   B. Flowers
      (Daisies) — $\begin{cases} \text{yellow tint} \\ \text{orange tint} \end{cases}$

3. A. Background — dark green (backgrounds)
   B. Flowers — $\begin{cases} \text{red tint} \\ \text{tones of white (small flowers)} \end{cases}$

4. A. Background — yellow ochre (backgrounds)
   B. Flowers — $\begin{cases} \text{blue tint} \\ \text{yellow tint} \end{cases}$

5. A. Background — light green (backgrounds)
   B. Flowers — $\begin{cases} \text{purple tint} \\ \text{yellow tint} \end{cases}$

LESSON TWO
LOBSTER AND WINE

Session I

After painting that *wild bouquet* and possibly some floral exercises, you are just about ready to try this still life. This painting was chosen for its *textures*: glass, porcelain, etc., not to mention that beady-eyed lobster, which is a real challenge! Don't groan. Just follow simplified directions. It is easier than you think.

FIGURE 1

The Drawing

1. Study the painting on page 52 and the completed drawing on page 53.

2. Use a small canvas (16″ × 20″ or approximate size). Use it vertically as for floral.

3. You have prepared the canvas as you did for the floral — stained with an umber wash and sectioned off. (*Note: All canvases are prepared in the same fashion.*)

4. Next, put in the drawing reduced to simple forms, again with the same umber wash and a **# 8** or **# 10 round sable brush.** Use **tissue** to *erase* if necessary. *Nearly always start placement at bottom of canvas.*

Next, decide *order of placement.* Naturally, the *bottle and jar* are *first* (background); then *lobster, butter cup* and *lemons* last. *Important: Notice where the light is coming from.* Note that *shadows* are on the *right*, so the *light* is coming from the *left*.

A. WINE BOTTLE

(1) We will start with bottle which will be put in a *box* for *correct size* and *placement.* (Study drawing and figure 1.) Draw a rectangle 7″ long and 3″ wide from line 4 to line 2 on line C. (*Note: The bottle is approximately 12 1/2 inches tall. These measurements may vary a little from drawing. This is just a general guide; don't worry.*)

(2) Go up *line C* from *line 2* about 5 1/2″ and put a dot — this is the top of the bottle.

(3) Now draw five *one-inch guidelines* across *line C*, as you see them in *figure 1.* Use grid lines as a guide.

(2) Next, draw *connecting vertical lines* back to box from these one-inch horizontal lines to form *cork, lip and neck of bottle. Caution:* Be sure to *curve both sides* of the bottle *the same.* (This takes a little doing.)

(5) Curve top and bottom of bottle, cork, lip, etc. downward, as if looking down on it. (See figure 1.)

(6) Put on label.

B. BLUE JAR

(1) Study painting on page 52 and drawing on page 53.
As the wine bottle *with line C*, the blue jar straddles line B. This aids in keeping sides uniform.
Note: The jar is about 1/2″ lower than wine bottle and is about 5″ tall.

(2) Draw a rectangle *5″ high and 3″ wide* from *1/2″ below line 4* to about *1″ above line 3 on line B.*

(3) See figure 2. Put in lines for lid and top of lid where indicated.

(4) Carefully curve top of lid. The top curve comes to small lines on

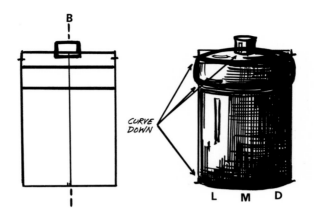

FIGURE 2

the sides.   The bottom curves up to meet it.   (The center is 1/2″ wide.)

(5)   As in the wine bottle, the *little round handle, lid and bottom of jar curve downward*.   (After wine bottle the blue jar should seem easier.)

C.   THE LOBSTER

This little critter may give you qualms.   Just follow directions and there he'll be.   Also *Italian lobsters* are *not* like our *Maine lobsters*.

(1)   Study painting on page 52 and drawing on page 53.
The lobster is about *3/4″ below blue jar*.   Without paper wrapper he is about 1″ from left edge of canvas.

(2)   Draw an oblong figure 2″ high and 7″ long.   It should come to line B.

(3)   Study *figure 3 carefully*.   (In the first stage he will look like a rocket.)
The *high point* is past the center on the top line and about 3/4″ high.
His *head* is about 2″ *long*.
Important: Remember his back tapers down and curls under, as shown. Also put claws in box.   And notice their placement and position.

(4)   The lobster is drawn in.   Now draw in the paper wrapper.   (Study drawing, page 53.)   It comes *over corner of jar* and lies *under his head* and goes off canvas on the *left side.   Keep the lines softly curved and lightly shade where indicated.*

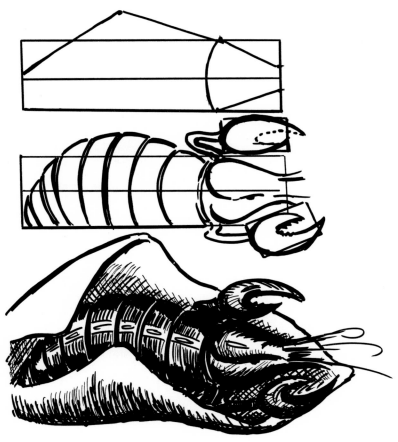

FIGURE 3

D. BUTTER CUP

  (1) Study painting on page 52 and drawing on page 53.
Draw a rectangle *2″ high and 3″ wide*. This rectangle overlaps into the corner of wine bottle 1 1/2″. Add base *2″ wide and 1/2″ high*. See figure 4.

  (2) *Curve top of rectangle* as shown (in perspective) *1/2″ down* on each side. The *lower* one is *curved up* to meet it; curve line of butter same as upper curve of cup.

  (3) Shape cup as shown, within box, and base also. Watch the downward curves. Shade lightly where indicated.

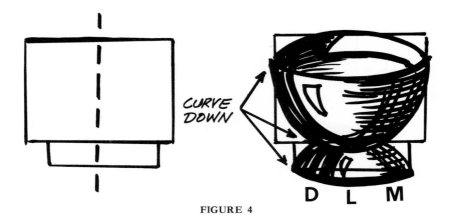

FIGURE 4

E. LEMONS

(1) Study painting on page 52 and drawing on page 53.
   Draw circles first, as indicated in *figure 5*.

(2) When properly placed, develop circles into lemons, as indicated.

(3) Remember the lemon halves must not be too small. When finished, lightly shade the uncut lemon (in shadow).

F. *Wipe out excess lines inside wine bottle, jar, etc.* Shade lightly, as indicated.
Also *indicate shadows under all objects quite definitely*. See completed drawing.

The drawing is finished. Clean brush and palette.

FIGURE 5

Now, let's paint!

Session II

The Background

1. Set up complete palette — see palette layout, page 7.

2. In this painting it is important to retain *dramatic tonal values.*

3. Consult *Chart for Background Color Combinations, page 24,* for tones of **dark green.** *Important:* (We are going to mix this a little differently.) *Mix* **medium tone** only. *Add to medium tone:* **3/4 teaspoon blue,** and **3/4 teaspoon purple** and **1 teaspoon aqua.** After these are mixed, follow the *directions* from chart for mixing the **light** and **dark tones** of **dark green background.**

4. After the above color is mixed, *remove* **3/4 teaspoon of dark tone** and *add:* **1/2 teaspoon purple, 1/4 teaspoon blue,** and **smidge of orange.** This is **extra-dark tone** for deep shadows around objects in painting.

5. Study painting on page 52 and drawing on page 53.

   A. Scoop up a little **dark tone.** (Nearly always start with dark tone.) Lightly paint with *flat of the knife* the left side of the canvas (to the paper of lobster). Use a *crisscross stroke*; don't load knife with paint. Clean knife.

Note: Do not touch center of painting around wine bottle for now.

   B. Scoop up some **medium tone** and again lightly paint, using the *same stroke*, the right side of canvas (to shadow on right). Check painting.

   C. Paint *area around bottle* with **light tone** as indicated in painting. Use clean knife to *lightly blend all three tones where they meet.* Use **extra-dark tone** you have put aside to put in *shadows* where you *see* them.

   E. Next, paint *foreground* and areas between shadows, **medium and light** in foreground, *blending the edges of shadows with background colors.* Again check painting. Clean knife.

   F. Finally, run your knife lightly through aqua (on palette) and stroke very thinly and lightly over **dark and medium tones** of *background.* (This creates an interesting effect.)

   The background is finished. Clean mixing area and knife.

1. Consult *Chart for Background Color Combinations* for tones of **burnt orange**. Mix color tones according to directions with *one exception: after mixing*, add **3/4 teaspoon** of **madder lake** to both the **medium tone** and the **dark tone**.

2. *Do not touch foil topping and cork for the moment.* Study figure 1 and the painting on page 52. Now, scoop up **dark tone** of **burnt orange** and paint right side of bottle. Try to use long flowing strokes. *Do not* let *strokes curve around* butter cup.)

3. Next, paint **dark tone** crosswise on bottom of the bottle, as indicated. Clean knife.

4. Scoop up **medium tone** (not too much) and lightly paint in middle tone. (Again, *do not curve strokes around label* — keep them *straight*.) *Remember, stroke denotes form.* Clean knife.

5. Next, paint in **light tone** where shown. (Watch strokes as they are clearly indicated in figure 1.) Clean knife. Blend some **dark tone** over the light tone on left edge of bottle. *Blend all tones only where they meet LIGHTLY.* Do not lose tonal values. Finally, stroke madder lake on the dark tone of bottle. Clean knife.

6. Pull aside **1/4 teaspoon light tone, add 1/2 teaspoon white** and smidge of **Naples yellow.** (This is the highlight on wine bottle. Do not use dead white.) Put on highlight where indicated.

7. Next, the *foil* and *cork on top* of bottle. Study painting, page 52. *Foil:* scoop up **straight yellow ochre,** and paint *right side* as indicated (delineate the lip of bottle). Clean knife.

8. Scoop up some **straight Naples yellow** and paint the *left side* of foil. (The foil is wrinkled, and so is uneven.) Clean knife.

9. *Cork:* paint *right side* of cork with **yellow ochre.** Next paint *top* and *left side* of cork with **Naples yellow.** Finally, scoop up some **madder lake** *and outline cork, across lip of bottle and down the right side of foil.* Go into the wrinkles a little.

The bottle is finished. Keep paint, if any. Clean mixing area and knife.

BLUE JAR

1. Consult *Chart for Basic Color Combinations* for *water color tones*. Mix according to directions.

2. After the three tones are mixed, take **1/2 teaspoon** of color from **light tone**; add **1/2 teaspoon white** and **smidge of Naples yellow.** Put aside for highlight.

3. Also take **1/2 teaspoon** of color from **dark tone,** add **1/2 teaspoon mixed green, 1/4 teaspoon purple, 1/4 teaspoon blue,** and a **smidge of orange.** This is the **extra-dark tone** used for *shadow* on jar.

4. Study painting and figure 2. Scoop up **dark tone** and paint in right side of jar. *Stroke color downward* and *across bottom* of jar. Use this same color to paint side of lid with a *horizontal stroke.* Paint small handle, as shown, and top of lid. Clean knife.

5. Paint in **medium tone** where indicated, using the same kind of stroke. Clean knife.

6. Paint **light tone,** as *shown in figure 2. Watch strokes.* Do not lose form. Clean knife.

7. Scoop up **extra-dark tone** and outline the *handle, lid, and right side of jar.* Work some of this tone on the *right side of jar.*

8. Now paint the *shadow of claw* on jar as you see it in painting, page 52, using *this same extra-dark tone.* Clean knife.

9. Finally, put the *highlight* where you see it in *painting* and drawing, using the *extra-light* tone put aside earlier.

   The jar is finished. Preserve paint if any. Clean mixing area and knife.

   Before tackling friend lobster, the painting should be put aside for a few days. Then you can attack the canvas with renewed *inspiration.*

Session III

1. *Paper Wrapper*

Note: The *wrapper* is painted first and then the lobster.

1. For the wrapper, consult *Chart for Mixtures of Color Tones* for **tones of white.** (These same tones will be used for butter cup.)   Mix according to directions. Study wrapper in figure 3.

2. Use the **dark tone of white** to paint under and around lobster, as shown.

3. *Shade* to **medium tone** underneath top fold of wrapper.   Clean knife.

4. Use the **light tone** to paint the white areas of wrapper.   On *top section* in *front of lobster, curve strokes* (see figure 3).   (There is a body in there.)

5. Add **dark tone** along *bottom of wrapper*, shading to **medium tone.**   *Blend* with **light tone** using *rounded strokes.*

6. Lightly work some *blue* from jar color into *dark areas of wrapper*.   Save remaining tones of white for butter cup.   Clean mixing area and knife.

Lobster

1. Study painting carefully.

2. Consult *Chart for Mixtures of Color Tones* for **tones of red.**   Mix according to directions.   After color is mixed, take **1/4 teaspoon of light tone** aside, add **1/2 teaspoon white** and **smidge of Naples yellow.**   This is **extra-light tone** for the *highlight* on his *nibs* (to be used last).

3. In studying figure 3 you will notice the shell of lobster is actually in *definite areas* of *tonal values*.   Do not overlook the formation of shell.   Study painting. Always remember to clean knife in going from one tone to another.

4. Paint **dark tone of red** *on top and bottom of body*.   Next, the **medium tone.** That *small area* in the *middle* is the **light tone.**   And on top of that is the **extra-light tone** for the highlight.
   Important: Watch strokes; they are in shape of body.

5. Paint **dark tone** of red on top and bottom of *head*.   See figure 3.   Next, put in the **medium tone,** then **light tone** in the middle and, as you can see, a highlight with **extra-light tone.**

6. Outline *head* in purple and *bring the line halfway around head* to *form eye*.   Also,

suggest little curved "feet" partially hidden by paper near head. Add "feelers" last. See figure 3.

6. *Claws* are mostly **dark and medium tone** (see painting), with light tone and highlight as shown.

7. The lobster is finished. Preserve any leftover paint. Clean mixing area and knife.

Butter Cup

1. Study painting carefully.

2. Use **tones of white** *previously mixed for paper wrapper.*

3. Use the **dark tone** to paint in *area on the left as indicated* in figure 4 (round stroke). Clean knife.

4. Use **light tone** to paint inside top of butter cup on the right, the *middle area on the cup front* and *the base.*

5. Use **medium tone** to paint the *right side of cup and base.* See figure 4. (Remember the *form* is the thing.) Blend tones lightly where they meet.

6. *Add highlights.* They will show, but very little.

7. Paint *butter* with **yellow ochre** for the *shadow area on left*, shading to **Naples yellow** on the *right inside cup.*

   The cup is finished. Clean mixing area and knife.

Lemons

1. Study painting, also figure 5.

2. The *whole lemon* is partially shadowed. Use **yellow ochre** *mixed* with a *little* **purple** to paint dark areas as indicated. Round object, round strokes. Go under navel.

3. Next with *straight cadmium yellow*, paint *middle tone*, as shown. Paint in *highlight*, as shown, of *zinc yellow mixed with a little white.* (Just a bloop.)

4. *Cut lemons.* Study figure 5. Again, use **ochre** mixed with **purple** to paint in **dark tone** *of shaded areas*, as indicated.

5. Then **middle tone of cadmium yellow,** and *highlight* of **zinc yellow** and **white.**

"I'M PAINTING THE LOBSTER FUCHSIA
TO MATCH MY DRAPES."

6. The inside of cut lemon is painted **white** *mixed with a smidge of* **mixed green.** Score it with clean knife, suggesting sections. Clean knife.

The painting is finished! Clean palette, knife, etc.

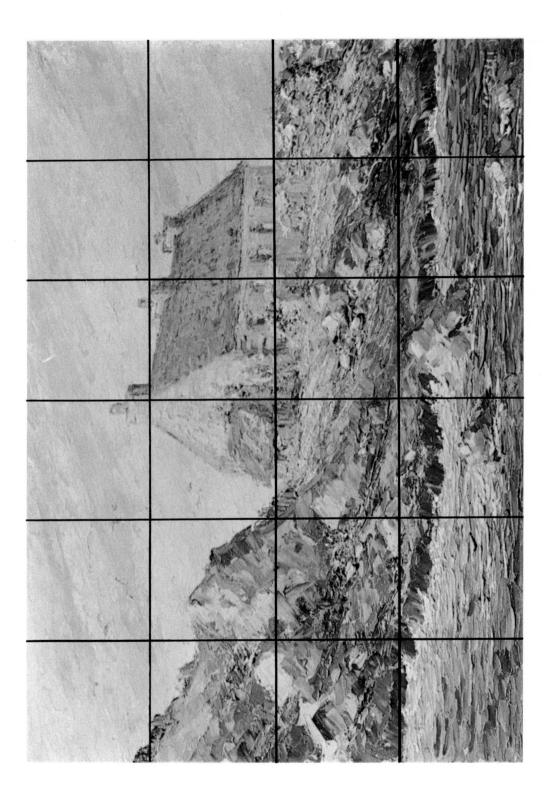

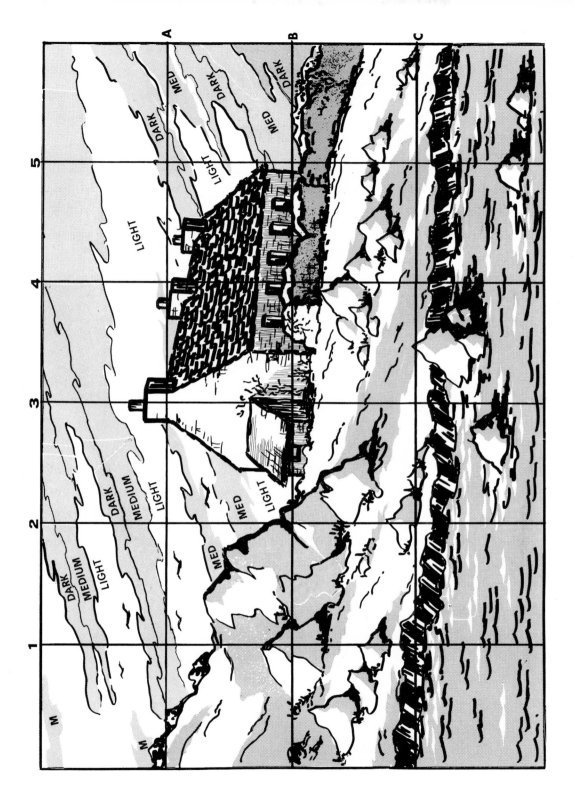

LESSON THREE
SCOTTISH SEACOAST

Session I

After doing a still life, you can now let yourself go with this exciting stormy seascape.

When you are finished with this painting, you can do a winter version with snow using the same composition, following the drawing and directions at the end of this lesson.

The Drawing

1. Study the painting carefully.

2. Use a canvas 18″ × 24″ or approximately that size.   Use it *horizontally*.   For this *seascape* your canvas is prepared in the usual way — umber wash and sectioned off (five vertical grid lines and three horizontal).   Use # **8** or # **10** **round sable brush** and umber wash as usual for drawing.

3. Study painting on page 66 and completed drawing on page 67.

    Note: The grid lines in drawing are numbered and lettered to facilitate drawing.

4. *Important: Always start by placing line for the horizon* (for seascapes, street scenes, landscapes, etc.).   The horizon in *this painting* is in *center of canvas*, but it is NOT *straight across* and so does *not cut picture in half*.

5. After horizon is drawn, follow grid lines and paint in the uneven *coastline*.

    A.   Start rocky hill on *line A* and draw it in.   Terrain is rough and uneven.
    B.   Study carefully rock formations before drawing rocks.   See drawing.
    C.   Carefully draw in the stone house, using the grid lines for correct placement and size.   See drawing.

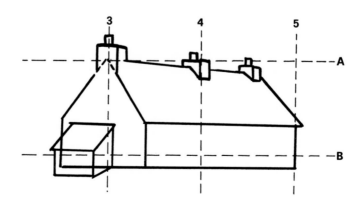

Important : Note slightly diminishing chimneys and sloping roof.   House in perspective.   Add details last (windows, vines, etc.).

D. Draw in broken stone wall as indicated in drawing.   (Note the thickness of broken wall.)

E. Draw rocks where indicated in sea.   *Don't have them in formation. Stagger* them and *please, no pointed croquet mallets.*   Check drawing.

F. *Study the sky carefully in drawing and section off your sky on canvas* likewise. This is a *complicated sky* and you *need all the help you can get.*

G. Since the *light is coming from the left, lightly shade all shadowed areas,* including the sea, as shown in completed drawing.

The drawing is finished.   Clean mixing area and brush.

Now, let's paint

Session II

Palette

1. Set up complete palette — see palette layout.

2. Usually the sky color is mixed and applied first. *The usual sky mixtures will not be used for this painting.*

3. In this painting, sky, house and wall are painted in the same tones — see painting.

4. Consult *Chart for Mixtures of Color Tones* for **tones of white.** Mix a *double batch* of color according to directions — with these additions:

   Light tone — *add extra*
   > **1/8 teaspoon Naples yellow**
   > **1/4 teaspoon orange**

   Medium tone — *add extra*
   > **1/4 teaspoon orange**
   > **1/4 teaspoon aqua**

   After tones are mixed, remove 3/4 teaspoon of dark tone. Add
   > **1/4 teaspoon aqua**
   > **1/4 teaspoon umber**
   > **1/4 teaspoon orange**

   This color is **extra-dark tone** for *roof, touches in sky* and *shadows on wall, chimneys, house,* etc.

Sky

1. Study painting and drawing.
   Note: In painting *sky* and *blending tonal values, knife must be cleaned constantly.*

2. Starting with **dark tone,** paint the *tones of the sky in designated areas* as shown in painting and drawing. *Do not load knife with paint.* Apply paint in a *slanting, lazy stroke* from *right corner to rocky hill in left corner.* Clean knife.

3. After all sky tones are in, with *clean knife, lightly blend tonal values where they meet,* using same slanting stroke. *Retain tonal values. Keep the horizon and area around front of house light.* (It's exciting to see the sky changing.)

4. *Don't overwork it. The sky is finished.* Clean knife, but not mixing area. House is next.

FIGURE 1

Patchwork stroke for house, roof, wall.

Stone House and Wall

1. *Note:* The sky tones will also be used for house and wall. Study painting and drawing.

2. *Important:* Remember, this is a *very old crumbling stone house.* Keep it very impressionistic.

3. *Paint house first,* then roof and wall.

4. Scoop up **dark tone** and with *small strokes (one across, one down,* etc. See figure 1) paint shadowed side of house. This stroke gives effect of stone to be used on house, wall and roof. (Here it looks like old tile.) Don't lose windows. Clean knife.

A. Use **medium tone** to paint *left side* of *front wall of house*, starting at the *top of chimney.*

B. Use **light tone** to paint the right side of this wall and around lean-to. *Important:* Notice the two tones are worked into each other to create stone effect. Clean knife.

C. Work some **extra-dark tone** on side of lean-to (rough texture) and shadow under this small roof. Also, put shadow of lean-to on house with **dark tone.** See drawing. Clean knife. Paint the lower part of *lean-to* and the front of the last two chimneys with **light tone.**

5. *Windows:* Use **extra-dark tone** to fill in top and left side of windows (not too definite, no detail). Clean knife. Now, use **light tone** to paint the *right side* of windows (the *opposite side*). Windows are *recessed* and *light does not turn corners.*

6. *Roofs:* Scoop up **extra-dark tone** and use *"patchwork"* strokes on the roof with knife (not too even). *Study painting.* Next, scoop up **dark tone** and work here and there over **extra-dark tone** on roof. (Have sides of roof uneven.)

A. *Small roof:* Underpaint with **medium tone** (very rough). Next, "patchwork" some **orange,** as shown, over **medium tone.** Put a few **light tones** on *right edge* of the *same roof.* Roof is finished.

B. Use **extra-dark tone** to paint *sides of all the chimneys.* Outline the *right* side of smaller chimneys. Next, put **orange** on the front of each small chimney.

7. *Wall:* Scoop up **dark tone** and with same strokes as used on the house, paint the shadowed side of wall. (*Important: leave area on top of wall.*) See drawing.

A. Next, work in some **extra-dark tone** here and there. Clean knife.

B. Use **medium tone** to paint *front of wall.* Also, work in some **light tone** here and there. (Remember old wall, yes?)

C. Use **light tone** to paint *top* of the *uneven wall.* Paint with **dark tone** where wall *dips* and *does not catch the light.* See drawing.

8. *House and wall are finished.* Hopefully they look like a *charming old ruin.* Preserve any leftover paint. Clean mixing area and knife.

A Word Between Sessions

The rocks are next.   At this point I'm tempted to say "ROCKS A RUCK!"   I won't say they are difficult, but tackle them after a brief respite.

Session III

Rocks

1. Study painting and drawing.

2. *Note:* The rocks will be painted in *mountain color (cool purple tones)* to preserve the *mood of the painting.*

3. Consult *Chart for Basic Color Combinations* for *mountain tones.* Mix according to directions, with this exception: **in medium tone reduce purple to 1/4 teaspoon.**
   After color is mixed, remove **1/2 teaspoon from light tone,** add **1/2 teaspoon white, 1/8 teaspoon** each **of Naples yellow** and **orange.** Set aside. This is **extra-light tone.**

4. *Study rock formation in drawing.* (It is very easy to have a uniform line of small pointed peaks — *don't.*)

FIGURE 2

5. Scoop up **dark tone** and paint *right side and bottom of rocks* where indicated. *Important*: Study form and character of rocks in drawing — *keep them craggy. Notice: In some instances, rocks in front shade those behind them (no light tone).*

6. Scoop up **medium tone** and paint in a *line of color along* **dark tone.**

7. Scoop up **light tone** and paint in *left side of rocks using flat downward stroke* (on an angle).

8. Use **extra-light tone** to paint those rocks catching more light (see painting), using same stroke as with light tone. Paint *all rocks, even those in water.* Clean knife.

9. Scoop up some **orange** paint and paint a few strokes in the dark areas — also some **aqua.** *The rocks are finished.* Preserve paint. Clean palette and knife.

Ground, Vines, etc.

1. Consult *Chart for Mixtures of Color Tones* for **tones of green.** Mix according to directions. After the color is mixed, remove **1/2 teaspoon of light tone** and add **3/4 teaspoon white, 1/2 teaspoon zinc yellow.** (This is extra-light tone.) Also remove **3/4 teaspoon of dark tone** and add **1/2 teaspoon purple** (for shadows of rocks in grass). Set both tones aside for last.

2. Study painting and drawing. Like the rocks, this *terrain has a special pattern and character. Everything in nature has its own pattern.*

3. The rocky hill on the left is in deep shadow. It's mostly medium and dark green, with a little light tone. Scoop up **medium green** and paint the color up into the rocks — they are buried in earth — and suggest vegetation growing between the rocks. You may even partially cover some of the rocks. *Study painting. No landscaping, please — it must be rough and wild.*

4. Painting the ground takes a special stroke. (See figure 2.) Scoop up **medium tone** and start painting from the rocks. Stroke paint toward coastline, but not straight. This gives the hill dimension.

5. Use this same interesting stroke to paint in the **medium** and **dark tones** where indicated. Use **light tone** on top of hill (on the left).

6. Use **extra-dark tone** to suggest taller vegetation on top of this same hill.

7. Now to ground surrounding house (bathed in light). This is painted in the **light** and **extra-light tones** and some **medium green.** Here the strokes

slant down to right as ground slopes. Again, it is uneven, rocky ground.

8. Study painting and paint the **light** and **extra-light tones** as you see them. Again, have vegetation growing between rocks.

9. Paint a delicate vine on the front wall — **dark green tone** in the shade, **light tone** in the sun. Paint vines on stone wall as indicated. They are neglected — wild and lovely.

10. Use **extra-dark green tone** to paint shadows under and on right side of rocks. *This wild interesting terrain is finished.* Preserve colors. Clean palette and knife.

Shoreline

1. The shoreline is uneven because of erosion. Study painting and drawing. *Notice:* Use the **dark** and **medium tones** of the rock colors (add **1/2 teaspoon of orange** to the **medium color**) and paint with *short slanting, downward strokes.*

2. Paint the **dark** and **medium tone** where indicated. Clean knife and mixing area.

The Sea

1. This choppy sea is mostly in deep shadow.

2. Consult *Chart for Basic Color Combinations* for **tones of water.** Mix according to directions, with one exception — to the **mixed dark tone** add **extra 1/4 teaspoon blue, 1/4 teaspoon orange** and **1/4 teaspoon thalo green.**

3. *Foam.* Remove **1/2 teaspoon light tone** from *sea color* and add **1/2 teaspoon white** and a **smidge Naples yellow.** Put aside.

4. *Note:* The **light tone** is along the shoreline, then the **medium tone** (very little) and the **dark tone.** Again, watch strokes. Study painting and drawing. Scoop up the **dark tone** and *paint where indicated*, using *short horizontal wavy stroke.*

5. Scoop up **medium tone** and *work it in with dark tone, but don't lose tonal values.* Clean knife.

6. Scoop up **light tone** and paint along shoreline, going into crevices, etc., as indicated. Put more **light tone** on the left part of sea.

7. Remember the rocks are obstructions, so the light tone splashes against them.

8. Apply foam along shore and into crevices, etc., on light tone against rocks and wherever indicated. Remember this is a choppy sea but not a violent one. Clean knife.

9. Stroke straight **purple** on sea, working it in behind rocks (shadow). Also stroke **purple** in foreground of the dark tone of the sea. Not too much — blend a little. *The sea is finished.* Clean mixing area and knife.

Sea Gulls

1. Study drawing of gulls (figure 3).

2. Mix two *distinct colors:*
   A. **1/4 teaspoon umber**   B. **1/4 teaspoon white**
      1/4 teaspoon blue   **Smidge Naples yellow**

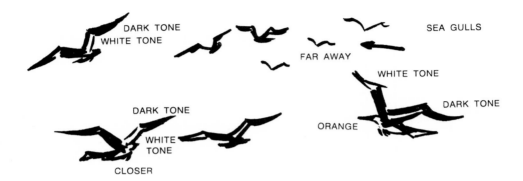

FIGURE 3

Not too well-defined. Keep them slender and graceful.
Varied sizes. Spot of orange in vicinity of beak.

3. Lightly draw in birds with **# 8** or **# 10 round sable brush.** Add color as indicated in drawing. The birds are no more than an inch long at most. Some are smaller — no vultures!

The painting is finished! It will most likely be one of your favorites. Before you get too relaxed, you can paint a "winter" version of the same composition.

EXERCISE
SCOTTISH SEACOAST: SNOW SCENE

Winter Version of Previously Painted Landscape

1. Repeat the drawing and painting of the previous project with the following exceptions and/or additions.
   A. No light tone on rocks — just snow.
   B. Naturally, no grass — ground covered with snow.
   C. Add snow on roofs — not too much — and on top of stone wall.

2. Consult *Chart for Mixtures of Color Tones* for **tones of white**. Remember, *these colors will look strange for snow*. Just follow directions and it will eventually make sense.

3. The **dark** and **medium tones** of *snow* are used on the *rocky hill* (on the left). *No short choppy strokes — same stroke as in grass previously.*

4. The **light tone** of snow used *around house*. **Dark tone** of snow on *large roof*, where indicated. **Light tone** of snow on small roof and chimneys.

5. For shadows of rocks on snow:
   Remove **1/2 teaspoon dark tone of snow**
   Add **1/4 teaspoon umber**
   1/4 teaspoon aqua
   This is **extra-dark tone.**

6. Even in snow scenes, highlights and shadows are essential.

This will be a charming painting. **The snow scene is finished.**

LESSON FOUR
ITALIAN FLOWER VENDOR

Session I

The best is saved for last. *Coraggio!* — you've come this far and survived. Admittedly, this is not an easy painting (as you may have already surmised). However, this painting has been greatly simplified, but will *definitely* take time. All those pots may do you in — but you will be pleased and proud with the results.

The Drawing

1. Study painting on page 80 and the completed drawing on page 81.

2. Use a 16″ × 20″ canvas or approximately that size. For this street scene, use it vertically.

3. Your canvas is prepared with an umber wash and sectioned off — five horizontal grid lines and three vertical.

4. Use the *horizontal* and *vertical grid lines* in the *completed drawing* as your *guide* (shown on page 81) and carefully put in your *drawing*. *Important:* The light is coming from the right — the shadows are on the left.

5. The actual drawing.
   A. *Block* in and *draw* the *building first*. Put in the *details last*.
   B. Next, draw in the *windows, doors,* and *shelf*. (Use the *grid lines* for *correct placement and size*.) See completed drawing.
   C. Draw in the *details on the roofs*.
   D. Now, draw in the *flower stall*. See figure 2. Add *pots and umbrella only*. *Notice:* The stall is about *2″ tall* and has *graduated shelves*.
   E. *Draw pots only* on shelves and wall. Draw boxes near doorways.
   F. Add *figures, vine, cat, lamp, and all flowers last*. It will be much easier than painting around them.
   G. *Lightly shade* areas for *shadows* as indicated in drawing, page 81.

6. *The drawing is finished.* Clean brushes and palette.

Now, let's paint!

1. Set up complete palette. (Don't squeeze out zinc yellow for now.) Put out *enough paint* and use *straight knife* for *mixing*. This painting was planned so that, with the exception of the flowers, you are actually using only *three mixed colors* which are repeated throughout the painting. *For example:* The *sky color* is also used for *shutters* and *umbrella*.

2. The color for the *building* and *street* will be mixed first. As you paint, it will be apparent why we did not mix the sky colors first.

3. Consult *Chart for Basic Color Combinations* for *earth tones*. Since this color is used in practically three-quarters of the painting, mix a *double batch of earth tones — light, medium, and dark*. Maintain distinct tonal values.

4. *Important:* After the three tones are mixed, remove **one teaspoon** of color from mixed **dark tone**. Add **1/2 teaspoon purple**. Mix and put aside. This is the **extra-dark tone** and is used for *shadows* of roof, shutters, shelf, etc. To the **light tone of earth color** add an extra **1/2 teaspoon of white** and **1/2 teaspoon Naples yellow** (for a brilliant sunlit effect).

Walls

1. Carefully study painting and completed drawing. Paint *one wall at a time*.
2. Wall 1.

    A. Start with *Wall 1 on the right side*. (Notice walls are numbered in drawing.) Mentally divide it in thirds and paint each section.

    B. Start with **dark tone** on the *right third of the wall*, then **middle tone** for *center section*, and **light tone** *for left section*.

    C. Use offset knife — do not load knife with paint — to paint in long, sweeping downward strokes, going around windows, doorways, shadows, etc. (*Blend tones only* where they *meet*.) Clean knife.

    D. Now, use **extra-dark tone** to paint shadows of *roof, shutters, shelf* and *top frame of curtained doorway*. Clean knife.

    E. Scoop up some **straight purple** from *palette* and paint *underside of roof, inside of windows* (carefully) and the *area between the curtains on doorway and also below each curtain*. See drawing, page 81. Clean knife. Now, with clean knife score the roof supports using the wet purple paint.

    F. Use the **light tone** to paint the frames of the windows, outlining the sills in **extra-dark tone**. See painting. That's all for the moment on Wall 1. Clean knife.

FIGURE 1

3. Wall 2.
   A. You will notice Wall 2 is in *deep shadow*, except for *side wall* in *upper left* which is painted in the **light tone,** as is the *ledge containing the plants.* (Light coming from the right.)
   B. Next, scoop up **dark tone** and *paint upper wall facing you.* Now, work in some **extra-dark tone** on the *right corner of this wall* — very little. Use same *extra-dark tone to paint shadows under roof.* Blend with *clean knife.*
   C. Paint *wall below* with **dark tone.** Use **extra-dark tone** *to shade corner,* going *around door and window and along bottom of the wall.* Blend lightly. Clean knife.
   D. Scoop up **middle tone** and *carefully paint doorframe* and inside the opening. See figure 1. Clean knife.
   E. Next, scoop up **light tone** — *very little* — and *highlight doorway.* Clean knife.
   F. Scoop up **straight purple** — very little — and shade *only top part* of opening of doorway. *Lightly* outline frame. Clean knife.
   G. Use **dark tone** to paint the right side of the small window frame where indicated. See figure 1. Clean knife.
   H. Paint the light side of the window frame with the **medium tone.** Clean knife.
   I. Now, use **straight purple** *to fill in the window opening.* Use *clean knife to scratch panes in wet paint.*

J.   Next, put a *shadow of purple under length of ledge with plants.* That's all for now for Wall 2. Clean knife.

4. Wall 3.   (Mentally divide in thirds and paint as in Wall 1.)

A.   Blend colors where they meet — don't lose *tonal values.*
B.   Use clean knife to scratch out "eyebrows" over each window.
C.   *Study* the *windows carefully* on this wall in the drawing on page 81.   You will notice there is an *inside line on the left sides only.*   Paint them in **the dark tone of earth color.**   Clean knife.
D.   Next, scoop up **light tone** and *very simply paint the facing around windows.*
E.   Fill window opening with **straight purple** — don't lose inner line. Clean knife.   *Note:* Work in a tiny bit of aqua over purple — and also in doorways, windows, and any place where solid purple is used.   This is for *accent.*
F.   *Study doorway* in figure 1.   As in *small window,* use **dark tone** on *the right side of frame* and **light tone** *on the left.*   *Paint purple in opening* and use clean knife to score sections in *wet purple.*   Clean knife.   *The buildings are finished — for the moment.*

5. *The Street*
    Note: There are *three definite areas of color.*   (Still use same earth tones.)

A.   Use the **extra-dark tone** *to paint the area in front of Walls 2 and 3 with long horizontal strokes,* where indicated, under flower stall, etc.   Clean knife.
B.   Next, use the **light tone** to paint the *middle area.*   Clean knife.
C.   Finally, use the **dark tone** to paint the third area.   Also *paint some dark tone in front of doorway.*   Blend tones — but don't lose *tonal values.*
D.   *Paint the boxes* by the *doorways in two tones — dark on the shade side (earth tones) and light on the front of boxes.*   Use **extra-dark tone** to put in *shadow* and *outline* the boxes *lightly* in purple.
E.   We are finished with the earth tones for now.   Put aside any leftover paint.   Clean mixing area and knife.   Cover palette with Saran Wrap.

A Word Between Sessions

It is advisable to wait a few days before going on to the next session.   This gives you a chance to recover a bit.   There's *lots* more to come!

Session II

Sky

1. Consult *Chart for Basic Color Combinations* for **sky tones** and mix according to directions. Use straight knife. *Note:* This color is used for the *sky, shutters, umbrella, and windowpanes.*

2. (Check completed drawing. You will notice the sky is divided into *three* areas.) Use **offset knife** to paint in the *top area* with **dark tone;** the *middle area* with **medium tone;** the *last area* in the **light tone,** going around buildings carefully. Clean knife.

3. *Starting* on the *left side of the sky* at the *line of building, drag the knife lightly upwards* through the *three tonal values* and *continue dragging with a clean knife* throughout the *sky colors, upwards each time,* until the sky is completed. *Not too much —* do not lose *tonal values. The sky is finished.*

Shutters, Umbrella, Windowpanes

1. *Shutters:* Paint all the shutters in the **dark tone only** of the *sky color.* Next, use a clean knife to *score the shutters* (suggesting *openings in shutters*).

2. *Umbrella:* Paint umbrella in **light and dark tones only** of the *sky colors.* Study figure 2. When painting umbrella, *preserve sections carefully* and *keep*

FIGURE 2

your strokes in shape of umbrella. Dark tones are on the left and *light tones are on the right.* Clean knife.

3. *Windowpanes:* Scoop a *little* **light tone** (sky) and *very lightly* suggest *glass in windows.* Also use **light tone** to paint some *wash hanging in top window — just a suggestion.* Use same *light tone* to put *some wash* in *box below* — as shown in painting — *very little.*

4. Move blue tones aside. Clean mixing area and knife.

Roofs, Curtains, Flowerpots

1. Consult *Chart for Background Color Combinations* for **tones of burnt orange.** Mix according to directions. This color is used for *roofs, curtain over doorway, and flowerpots on wall.*

DARK   LIGHT

FIGURE 3

2. *Roofs on Walls 1 and 3 have the same treatment.* Study figure 3. The two roofs are painted in **dark and light tones of burnt orange** only.
   A. The paint is applied in *short strokes* along *edge of roofs* (as shown in figure 3) *alternately* in *light and dark tones.* Slant them and keep them low.
   B. *Roof* on *Wall 2* is painted first in *three tonal values* — **dark tone** on the *right* corner, then **medium tone,** then the **light tone** on the *corner of roof* (catching the light). Clean knife.
   C. Paint a little *purple tone lightly* over *dark tone in corner* (deep shadow). Clean knife.
   D. After paint is applied, *scallop top and bottom of roof* as shown in figure 3. *Score it with a clean knife* — first *vertically* in *long lines,* suggesting *sections,* and then each section with *curved lines.* (This suggests a *heavy tile roof typical in Italy.*) *Do not attempt to draw tiles separately. The roofs are finished.*

3. *Doorway drapes* are painted in **light and dark tones of burnt orange.**
   A. Scoop up **dark tone** and paint in dark folds of drapes on the *left* (as shown in figure 1). Light is coming from the right. Clean knife.
   B. Paint **light tone** on folds on the *right*. *Put a few strokes in between light folds.*
   C. Next, use *purple color* to stroke in a kind of scallop at the top of drapes to suggest folds (see figure 1) and also at the bottom of drapes.
4. Finally, put in *chimney*. Use **dark tone of burnt orange** and add **straight purple** on the *shade side*.

FIGURE 4

5. *Flowerpots* are painted in **light and dark tones of burnt orange.** The **dark tone** is painted on the *left side and bottoms of pots* and the *light tone* is on the *right*. Put a *purple shadow* on *left behind pots* (as shown in figure 4).

6. Move paint. Clean mixing area and knife.

Foliage for pots, vine, etc.

1. Consult color *Chart for Mixtures of Color Tones* for **tones of green.** Mix according to directions. After color is mixed, remove **1/2 teaspoon** from

dark tone and add **1/4 teaspoon of purple.** Mix and *put aside for extra-dark green.* (This is used to paint the pots on the flower stall.)

2. Paint the *pots on the stall* **extra-dark green** *on left sides and bottoms.* Paint **medium green** on the *right sides.*

3. Paint a graceful vine (without foliage) of *purple* in corner of Wall 2 and over door. (See completed drawing.) Clean knife.

4. Now, let's put the greenery in the pots and on the vine, etc. Study figure 4. Scoop up **dark tone of green** and lightly blot leaves on left side in pots on shelf. Very little and lacy — no bushes, please. Next, paint a few light green leaves on the right side. Add geraniums later.

5. Do the same with all pots on ledge Wall 3, as shown in figure 4.

6. Paint *leaves on vine* in **medium and dark tones** (vine in shadow) with a few *light green* leaves over doorway — *very lacy* and *delicate.* (Just blot it on lightly with flat of knife.)

7. Add some *greenery in box near stall* — *tall and delicate. Dark tone* on the *left, light tone* on the *right.* (See figure 2.) Also add some *greenery* (see painting) *in pots at top of flower stall* and where seen in the same way. Preserve any leftover paint. Clean mixing area and knife.

8. Again, take a breather and wait a few days before resuming.

Session III

Flowers

1. *Geraniums*
   A. These are quite simple to paint.   They are in pots on shelf and ledge.
   B. Paint *blobs* (small) each **1/2 vermilion** and **1/2 orange** — not too many — among greenery.   (See figure 4.)

2. Study flowers on the stall.   They are partly in shadow under the umbrella. Each bouquet is painted *1/2 dark and 1/2 light of each color*.   Those in *shadow* are *not as bright*, and are the following mixtures:

> **madder lake** and **vermilion**
> **ochre** and **cadmium yellow medium**
> **blue** and **aqua,** etc.

For those bouquets *catching the light*, you *simply add white for the light tone* (*i.e.,* vermilion and white for the light tone).   Do the same for *cadmium yellow medium*, *aqua*, *blue*, etc.   Or you can make your own combinations.   But, to be effective, be conscious of *light* and *shadow*.

People

1. *Don't panic*.   Study figure 5 carefully.   Before you attempt the women on canvas do a few practice figures first.   You will notice the larger woman is broken down in squares.   She is 2 3/4" tall; from top of head to waist 1"; waist to skirt 1"; and the legs are 3/4" long.   Don't make the head too large.

FIGURE 5

2. The small figure in the doorway is 1 1/2″ tall and rather vague.

3. With a **# 8 round sable brush** and **umber** paint draw figures carefully where indicated.

4. Next, scoop up *straight purple* with knife — the figures are almost silhouetted — and carefully paint in the figures. Highlight the larger woman (see figure 5) with *orange*. Lightly outline figure in doorway with a little *aqua*.

Lantern, Cat, Birds

1. Lightly paint the *small lantern* by the door on Wall 1 with *purple*.

2. Paint in the *cat* with *purple*, but be careful — he can so easily look like a rodent or rabbit.

3. And finally (sigh), paint in the *birds*. (Use **# 8 round sable brush** and **umber**; paint *not too dark*.) Birds must be *graceful* and *delicate*. (Please — no eagles.) Be careful not to put in too many birds.

The painting is finished. Bravo! This was a complicated and detailed painting, and it was a great challenge. And, after all, you wouldn't want to paint flowers all the time!...or would you? Although — a very posh interior decorator who attended an art exhibit absolutely flipped over a fantastic painting of strawberries. She was so excited that she arranged to see more of the artist's work. But when she entered the artist's home and saw the other paintings she could not believe her eyes. Every room was covered with wall-to-wall paintings of strawberries — strawberries and nothing but strawberries — that was it! The decorator left in a state of shock.